WOMEN'S AND CHILDREN'S FASHIONS OF 1917

The Complete Perry, Dame & Co. Catalog

❄

PERRY, DAME & CO.

DOVER PUBLICATIONS, INC.
NEW YORK

Copyright © 1992 by Dover Publications, Inc.
All rights reserved under Pan American and International Copyright Conventions.

Published in Canada by General Publishing Company, Ltd., 30 Lesmill Road, Don Mills, Toronto, Ontario.

Published in the United Kingdom by Constable and Company, Ltd., 3 The Lanchesters, 162–164 Fulham Palace Road, London W6 9ER.

This Dover edition, first published in 1992, is a complete, unabridged reprint of *Catalog No. 67, New York Styles, Spring and Summer 1917* as published by Perry, Dame & Co., New York City. A new Publisher's Note has been written specially for the present edition. Plates originally in color are here reproduced in black and white, except for those on the inside covers.

Manufactured in the United States of America
Dover Publications, Inc., 31 East 2nd Street, Mineola, N.Y. 11501

Library of Congress Cataloging-in-Publication Data

New York styles, spring and summer 1917.
    Women's and children's fashions of 1917 : the complete Perry, Dame & Co. catalog / Perry, Dame & Co.
        p.   cm.
    "Complete, unabridged reprint of catalog no. 67, New York styles, spring and summer 1917, as published by Perry, Dame & Co., New York City"—T.p. verso.
    ISBN 0-486-27128-5 (pbk.)
    1. Costume—United States—History—20th century—Catalogs. 2. Perry, Dame & Co.—Catalogs. I. Perry, Dame & Co. II. Title.
GT615.N48   1992
391'.0074'7471—dc20   92-12621
                                                       CIP

Publisher's Note, 1992

Mail order existed in rudimentary form as early as the 1830s; it was Montgomery Ward, with its catalog of 1872, that began the huge industry that continues to this day. Making available to farmers and other rural folk goods and fashions substantially the same as those being sold in metropolitan areas, mail-order firms proliferated.

While firms such as Montgomery Ward and Sears, Roebuck sold a staggering variety of goods—from clothing and books to farm equipment and plumbing supplies—others were more limited in their offerings. Perry, Dame & Co. was such a business, stating in its Catalog No. 67, *New York Styles, Spring and Summer 1917* (reproduced here), that "We Sell by Mail Women's, Misses' and Children's Wearing Apparel Only." The catalog has many of the features found in those of larger companies—the emphasis on high quality, low price and complete reliability of service. But while Sears extended an invitation to its customers visiting Chicago to tour its operation, Perry, Dame, at 142–154 East 32 Street, New York, did not.

The clothing shown in the catalog reflects popular rather than high fashion, although the fashions are far from dowdy. The trend was toward simplicity and freedom of movement. The house dress was a popular garment; the hobble skirt, introduced in 1911, had passed from the scene. Generally, fashions reveal a simple silhouette with rich fabrication and detailing featuring a great variety of belts, the application of buttons and trim (with a good deal of eyelet embroidery) and large collars (including the V-neck, which had originally been denounced as immoral). Traces of an earlier fashion—the tunic top worn over an underskirt—are still to be seen in the catalog. The waist is usually high, and the hem is above the ankle, revealing shoes, sometimes high-buttoned, with pointed toes and French heels. Wide-brimmed hats with elaborate trimming predominate; it was in part because of the necessities of riding in an open motorcar that they were later simplified. Other features worth noting are belted sweaters and elegant, pencil-thin umbrellas.

It is probable that this catalog had been published before the United States declared war on Germany in April 1917. After the armistice, there was a brief attempt to return to the styles of ca. 1915–16, but fashion soon resumed its evolution, starting a new cycle that culminated in the famous costumes of the mid-twenties.

WOMEN'S AND CHILDREN'S FASHIONS OF 1917

New York Styles
Spring and
Summer
1917

PERRY, DAME & CO.
NEW YORK CITY

Catalog No. 67

[original front cover]

A Guarantee

A Perry-Dame customer gets exactly what she buys. Clothes that are exactly as shown in the pictures. Quality exactly as represented. Value she has a right to expect. Care and promptness in shipping the goods. THE GUARANTEE OF AN ESTABLISHED AND RESPONSIBLE FIRM.

You must be pleased in your dealings with the established house of Perry, Dame & Co., in every way. If the garment you buy is not all that you have a right to expect—and you must be the judge after examining it—we Guarantee to promptly refund your money and pay the cost of returning the goods, without one cent of expense to you.

It is the honest, straightforward, exact showing of the garments in this catalog, with the detailed descriptions of the styles and materials shown by the pictures, that has built this great and successful Mail Order firm of Perry, Dame & Co.

We say every customer must be satisfied.

We offer you the best material and workmanship, the latest, most attractive and seasonable styles at the lowest possible prices.

We give you our assurance, emphasized by our guarantee on every purchase, of absolute satisfaction or your money back.

Perry, Dame & Co.

"A BLAZE OF COLOR" IS FASHION'S VERDICT THIS SEASON

Dame Fashion has this season gathered together all the rich colorings of the Far East and blended them into garments of exquisite beauty.

In this book we offer you the latest style dresses in every rich shade and in every popular material demanded by Fashion for the Spring and Summer.

An Exquisite Gown of Newest Style

1A3—Charming Frock of Superior Quality Taffeta combined with Fine Georgette Crêpe. The demand for metallic trimming is satisfied in the design on the collar and tunic skirt, which is embroidered in gold thread. The low neck and transparent sleeves make this gown appropriate for dress occasions. The Taffeta belt and the cuffs are trimmed with fancy buttons. *Colors:* Gray, gold, bisque or national blue. *Sizes:* 32 to 46 bust measure.. **$19.75**
1A203—Same style and colors as No. 1A3 but made in Misses' and Small Women's sizes 14 to 20 years........ **$19.75**

IA3
IA203
$19.75

New Model Dress of Marquisette

1A402—Delightful Afternoon Dress of Marquisette. Excellence of material and workmanship characterize this model. Fine shadow lace supplies the collar and the dainty vestee. Soft Messaline Silk is used for the belt, which is pointed at the front. Messaline appears again as a piping on the long sleeves and as loops and buttons on the waist and pouch pockets. Two of these attractive pockets are seen on the gathered skirt. Two plaits extend around the skirt immediately below the pockets. *Colors:* Rose, green or blue, predominating and trimmed to match. *Sizes:* 32 to 46 bust measure........... **$6.98**

IA402
$6.98

IA403
IA603
$8.98

1A403—Dress of Colored Voile. Back and front alike. Sheer organdie collar and button trimmed vestee hemstitched and edged with Val. Crocheted buttons trim the revers. Side plaited waist. Box plaited skirt sections afford pleasing grace. Horizontal plaits on side gores. *Colors:* Flesh, lavender or maize. *Sizes:* 32 to 46 bust...... **$8.98**
1A603—Same style and colors as No. 1A403 but made in Misses' and Small Women's sizes 14 to 20 years .. **$8.98**

IA6
IA206
$6.98

IA5
$15.98

1A6—Dress of Superior Quality Striped Silk Pongee. Perfectly blended stripes and figures in contrasting colors on a natural colored pongee background. Pearl buttons trim the front closing and the patch pockets. Deep collar and cuffs of Sand Colored Satin. Graceful side plaited skirt. *Sizes;* 32 to 46 bust. *Colors:* As pictured only... **$6.98**
1A206—Same style and colors as No. 1A6, but made in Misses' and Small Women's sizes 14 to 20 years... **$6.98**

1A5—Finely Made Afternoon Dress of Soft Silk Crêpe de Chine. The panels, front and back, achieve long, graceful lines. Fine silver threads trace an embroidered design around the neck and on the front panel. Long sleeves have flare cuffs. Three deep plaits on each side of the skirt. Invisible side closing. *Colors:* Navy blue, black or gray. *Sizes:* 32 to 46 inches bust measure. **$15.98**

1A4—Smartly Designed Dress of Soft Chiffon Taffeta. Beautifully hand-embroidered with bright colors on the waist front and cuffs. New "throw-tie" girdle encircles the waist. The deep pointed overskirt contributes desirable length of line. Silk Poplin collar. *Colors:* Sapphire blue, black or apple green. *Sizes:* 32 to 46 bust......... **$9.98**
1A204—Same style and colors as No. 1A4 but made in Misses' and Small Women's sizes 14 to 20 years. **$9.98**

IA4
IA204
$9.98

1A409—Beautiful Frock of Handsomely Embroidered White Net, trimmed with Filet Pattern Lace. The Crushed Satin Ribbon Girdle comes in white and maize, white and blue or white and pink. The collar is inset with Filet Pattern Lace and finished with a picot edged net ruffle. Embroidered net forms a bolero effect on the waist front where it is outlined with Filet insertion and a pin-tucked net chemisette. The Chemisette crosses in surplice fashion and is finished with crocheted ball trimming. The back of waist is also trimmed with the embroidered net and Filet insertions. The deep cuffs are of pin-tucked net inset with Filet lace and completed with a picot edged net ruffle. The richly Embroidered Net Panniere Tunic is made over a net underskirt. It is outlined front and back by the panels of gathered net trimmed with wide Filet insertions and bordered with a row of hemstitching. *Sizes: 32 to 46 bust measure.* **$13.98**

1A609—Same as 1A409, but in small women's and misses' sizes...... **$13.98**

1A408
$7⁹⁸
FLORAL
LACE CLOTH

1A408—Dainty Dress of Floral Lace Cloth, a cool Summer dress material. The yoke, armholes and cuffs are hemstitched. Collar, cuffs and bands at waist of soft Satin Messaline. Silk Radium Lace extends from the collar to the belt and is trimmed with fancy buttons and Messaline. The skirt is a gracefully gathered model and falls softly from the shirrings at belt, which is finished with a frill. Three narrow ruffles appear above the hem. *Colors:* Biscuit with Copenhagen, green with rose, or lavender with lavender Messaline. *Sizes: 32 to 46 bust measure.* **$7.98**

1A409
1A609
$13⁹⁸
EMBROIDERED NET
WITH
FILET PATTERN
LACE

1A10
$14⁹⁸
TAFFETA SILK
WITH
GEORGETTE
CRÊPE

Skirt Lengths of Women's Dresses are 40 inches, with a deep basted hem for easy adjustment.

1A10—New Model Dress of Soft Chiffon Taffeta combined with Georgette Crêpe. The Georgette supplies the waist, which is made over a foundation of lace-trimmed net and Paisley Pattern Art Silk which shows through the Georgette. The armholes are outlined with hemstitching and the cuffs of the sleeves are banded with the Chiffon Taffeta. The vogue for metallic embroidery is displayed on the revers and on the collar of white Georgette, finished with a piping of the Taffeta. The skirt falls in soft folds from below the belt. On the side gores a gathered section with a heading of the material is introduced and finished at the bottom, above the hem, with two rows of cording. *Colors:* National blue, gray or green. *Sizes: 32 to 46 bust.* **$14.9**

Remarkable Offering of New Style Dresses

1A616—Same Costume as 1A416 but in Misses' and Small Women's sizes.. **$7.98**

1A414
$4.29
FLORAL
CREPE

1A415
$6.98
STRIPED
VOILE

1A416
1A616
$7.98
SPORT
CREPE

1A414—A Charming Dress of Floral Crêpe, artfully combined with Snowflake Net. The net supplies the sleeves and the underblouse, which is outlined both front and back by the floral crêpe, cut in novel outline. A smart embroidered collar completes the neck. Two-toned crotcheted buttons trim the invisible front closing. The belt of the material is finished with a loop and slashed ends. The tunic skirt is softly gathered at the waist and finished with a corded hem. *Colors:* Copenhagen, lavender or apple green on white ground. *Sizes:* 32 to 46 bust measure.............. **$4.29**

1A415—One of the Season's Smartest Dresses, cleverly fashioned from plain and striped voile in colors to match. The collar, revers and cuffs are of finely embroidered organdie, stitched in contrasting color. Three deep plaits over the shoulders, stitched to bust depth, secure necessary fulness for the waist front. The graceful tunic skirt is laid in soft folds, the upper and lower portions being completed by applied hems of the solid color material. Soft satin girdle at waist to match. *Colors:* Navy, black or Copenhagen stripes combined with white. *Sizes:* 32 to 46 bust.... **$6.98**

1A416—A Handsome, Carefully Tailored Costume of Finest Quality Sport Crêpe. For wear with or without a blouse. In accord with the demand for colors, the deep collar, vest, cuffs and patch pockets are of bright colored crêpe—an effective contrast to the snowy white material. New style belted flare coat. Slot seam at back achieves a neat appearance. Inverted hem at bottom and side front of coat. Large pearl button closing. Cleverly designed bell shaped skirt—the very latest vogue. *Colors:* White with apple green, rose or gold. *Sizes:* 32 to 46 bust............................... **$7.98**

Moderately Priced Dresses for Afternoon and Evening Wear

1A12—Evening Dress of Soft Silk Messaline. The soft folds of the silk bodice and the plaited folds of the fine shadow lace are made over a foundation of firm white net. The shoulder straps and the cuffs of the sleeves are of the Silk Messaline. The corsage bouquet is of roses, silk leaves and mignonette to contrast with the delicate colors of the novelty silk and gold banding which trims the upper portion of the waist. The two-section skirt is made with a softly gathered yoke and a flounce set off with a shirred heading at the top and three rows of cording at the bottom. *Colors:* Flesh, white, maize or light blue. *Sizes:* 32 to 46 bust measure **$9.98**

1A212—Same as 1A12, but in small women's and misses' sizes **$9.98**

1A417
1A617
$5.98
EMBROIDERED VOILE

1A418
1A618
$8.98
EMBROIDERED VOILE

1A12
1A212
$9.98
SILK MESSALINE

1A417—Afternoon Dress of Richly Embroidered Voile in Solid and Eyelet Design. The body of the waist is of embroidered Voile and is trimmed with a deep collar of embroidered Organdie edged with a hemstitched net ruffle. The vestee is of shirred and hemstitched net, finished with ball trimming. Sleeves of plain voile, with a plait above the elbow and trimmed with cuffs of the same materials as the collar. The graceful skirt is of the embroidered voile. The belt in rose, maize or white is finished with a smart bow. *Sizes:* 32 to 46 bust measure **$5.98**

1A617—Same as 1A417, but in small women's and misses' sizes **$5.98**

1A418—Dainty Loose Fitting Dress of Finely Embroidered Voile, over a firm net waist foundation. The embroidered design is in a color to match the Silk Rope Girdle. Outlined with hemstitching, the embroidered voile supplies the collar and the trimming around the neck and down the waist front. Yoke plaits in back. The embroidered cuffs are hemstitched. The skirt falls in side plaits and has a deep embroidered section above the hem. *Colors:* All white, or white embroidered in rose or blue. *Sizes:* 32 to 46 bust. **$8.98**

1A618—Same as 1A418, but in small women's and misses' sizes . . **$8.98**

A New Style Dress of Distinction

and a Dress of Unusual Charm

1A410
$6.98
FLORAL
VOILE

1A11
$12.98
TAFFETA SILK
WITH
GEORGETTE
CRÊPE

1A410—A Beautiful Summer Dress of Fine Floral Voile, cleverly fashioned on Colonial lines and made with a black velvet lacing at the front bodice. Tiny ruffles of plain white outlined with rows of fancy stitching ornament the dainty collar. The pin-plaited chemisette of plain white voile at the front is finished with rows of cording and a band of thread lace insertion at the top. Corded white voile also binds the bottom of the bodice and the edge of the sleeve, above the stitched ruffles of white voile. The skirt is made with pleasing fulness. Two deep plaits appear below hip depth and three above the hem. They encircle the back of the skirt and terminate at either side of the front. Invisible side front closing. *Colors:* Rose combination or blue combination, each trimmed with white as described. *Sizes:* 32 to 46 bust measure.. $6.98

1A11—A Smart Appearing, Carefully Made Dress of Soft Chiffon Taffeta. Designed with a deep pointed Tunic, suggestive of long, slender lines. The front closing is effected with taffeta corded loops and covered buttons. The waist is made over a fine white lawn lining, trimmed with a hemstitched picot-edged collar of white taffeta. The sleeves are of Georgette Crêpe, finished with Taffeta Cuffs. *Colors:* Navy, black or gray, trimmed as described. *Sizes:* 32 to 46 bust measure.. $12.98

1A413—New Model Sport Costume. The waist portion is in Redingote Fashion of Mercerized Checked Crêpe, with collar and cuffs of hemstitched white French Linon. Tasseled mercerized cord in colors to match distributes the fulness. Plain gored skirt of white French Linon is attached to a lawn waist lining. *Colors:* Gold and white, apple green and white or Copenhagen and white. *Sizes:* 32 to 46 bust measure... **$5.98**

1A613—Same as 1A413, but in small women's and misses' sizes, 14 to 20 years.... **$5.98**

**1A412
1A612
$4.98
TUB
GABARDINE**

Skirt Lengths of Women's Dresses are 40 inches, with a deep basted hem for easy adjustment.

**1A411
$7.98
EMB. VOILE**

**1A413
1A613
$5.98
MERCERIZED
CRÊPE
WITH
FRENCH
LINON**

1A411—Dress of Soft White Voile, embroidered in a handsome flower design. Crocheted buttons trim the box plaits of the waist above the front closing. Lace insertions trim the collar and cuffs. The sleeves are cut in points at the elbow, above which the voile is plaited. The Embroidered Voile overskirt is laid in folds beneath the silk girdle. On the side gores are new pendant pockets of lace trimmed with crocheted buttons. The skirt is plain voile, trimmed with plaits and lace insertion. *Sizes:* 32 to 46 bust. *Colors:* White with white, light blue or maize girdle................. **$7.98**

1A412—Smart, Trim Appearing Dress of White Tub Gabardine. The collar and shallow cuffs over the deep gabardine cuffs of the long sleeves, are of picot-edged tan linen, which also pipes the new model patch pockets. The belt across back terminates at the front panel which is trimmed with pearl buttons and soutache braid. Similar braid trims the pockets of the plain gored skirt. *Sizes:* 32 to 46 bust measure............. **$4.98**

1A612—Same as 1A412, but in small women's and misses' sizes, 14 to 20 years..... **$4.98**

WE PREPAY ALL DELIVERY CHARGES

9

1A8—Tussah Silk Sport Costume. Waist lining of white lawn, to which the skirt is stitched. Deep pointed collar, cuffs, and the hems of the waist and skirt finished with bands of Cubist figured Tussah. In front, side plaits are laid below yoke. "Throw-tie" belt completed with figured material. Novelty button closing. Side plaited skirt. *Colors:* Tan, rose or Copenhagen. *Sizes:* 32 to 46 bust...... **$6.49**

1A407
$2⁵⁹
Voile

Specially Priced Crêpe de Chine Dress at $10.98

1A9—Smart Afternoon Dress of Soft Silk Crêpe de Chine. Below the yoke, both front and back, the waist falls in soft box-plaited folds which are continued to the hem of the graceful skirt. The cuffs are of white silk Crêpe de Chine to match the collar, which is completed by a slip-knot tie in contrasting color. Smooth fitting lining forms the waist foundation. An embroidered worsted design trims both the front and back of belt. *Colors:* Navy, black or tan. *Sizes:* 32 to 46 bust measure...... **$10.98**

1A8
$6⁴⁹
Tussah Silk

1A406—Dress of Figured Voile. Corded belt, collar, cuffs and skirt trimmed with ruffles. Collar has an overlay of hem-stitched net which continues down the front as a vestee, trimmed with buttons. White lined waist. *Colors:* Copenhagen, lavender or gold. *Sizes:* 32 to 46 bust.. **$3.69**

1A407—Dress of Figured Voile. Gathers beneath shoulder yoke. Closes through lace-trimmed front panel. Cuffs and collar of white voile hemstitched with black. Gathered skirt yoke extends down front in a panel. From either side of panel the material, cut cross-wise, forms a flounce. *Colors:* Black, rose or Copenhagen. *Sizes:* 32 to 46 bust............... **$2.59**

1A406
$3⁶⁹
Voile

1A9
$10⁹⁸
Silk Crêpe de Chine

Stylish Dresses Especially Designed for Stout Figures

A Beautiful Taffeta Silk Dress

1A7—Good Looking Afternoon Dress of Soft Chiffon Taffeta. Modelled on long straight lines to give a slender appearance to above-the-average figures. The collar, revers, cuffs and belt are of the Taffeta with a satin stripe. Tiny pearl buttons trim the soft Georgette Silk waist front. *Colors:* All black or navy with contrasting colored silk. *Sizes:* 39 to 53 bust............................ **$13.98**

1A405
$5.98
Pongee

1A404
$4.69
Embroidered
Voile

1A7
$13.98
Taffeta Silk

Perry-Dame Dresses for Stout Figures come 41 inches long, with a deep basted hem for easy adjustment.

1A404—Beautiful Dress of Embroidered Voile, trimmed with Organdie and thread lace. Thread lace in double rows trims the Organdie collar. Hemstitching outlines the vestee bordered at each side with the embroidered voile. The back of waist is plain, except for triple rows of pin tucking. The three-quarter sleeves are of the embroidered voile. Two section skirt inset with embroidered voile between plaits. Soft silk girdle. *Colors:* All white, or white and black. *Sizes:* 39 to 53 bust... **$4.69**

1A405—Neatly Made Dress of Striped Cotton Pongee. Designed for women above the average figure. The striped material is conducive to long, slender lines. The gathered net chemisette has ribbon-run beading. It terminates in a panel of plain colored pongee with tiny pearl buttons. Plain colored material supplies the neat belt at sides and back. It also trims the collar, cuffs, and the well proportioned, slightly flared skirt. *Colors:* Tan and rose or tan and Copenhagen. *Sizes:* 39 to 53 bust.......... **$5.98**

SEE COMPLETE INDEX ON PAGE 125

The Right Dresses For The Right Times & Places

It will pay you to give these pages the most careful consideration.

There is something in them for every woman's needs.

We say to you that the styles shown are the very latest—right up to the minute. They are bound to be wonderfully popular. You will agree that the patterns, designs and colors are beautiful.

And remember this, you will find in every garment, whether it be morning dress, afternoon dress, evening dress, or one of those stunning sport models, quality of the highest order.

Description of the Beautiful New Style Afternoon Costume Shown on this Page

1A26—A Beautiful Afternoon Costume of High Grade Faille Silk, made in three-piece effect. The deep collar, revers and front facing of the coat are of contrasting colored material. The loose fitting coat is made without sleeves, making it easier to slip on and, at the same time, procure an entirely different effect. The waist portion of the dress is made with a stitched collar, front vestee and cuffs of the contrasting colored material. At either side of the front stitched box plaits relieve all tendency toward severity. The waist lining is of firm white muslin, edged at the neck with narrow lace. The skirt is cut with just the proper flare. It is fastened to the waist with two rows of cording and a narrow heading of the material. A single row of cording lends an attractive touch to the lower skirt portion. *Colors:* Steel gray and rose, navy and tan, tan and Copenhagen, or black and white. *Sizes:* 32 to 46 bust measure... **$10.98**

1A226—The same material and colors in small women's and misses' sizes: 14 to 20 years.............................. **$10.98**

This new "Sleeveless Coat" Costume is the very last word in Women's Wearing Apparel. It is made of one of the season's most popular materials in the newest colors.

How to Order Your Right Size Dress

Ladies' dresses come in sizes 32 to 46 bust with a skirt 40 inches in length. Made with a deep basted hem so they can be easily shortened or lengthened by the customer, if so desired. Send us your actual waist and bust measures and we will send you the right size. If you wish, you may also send us your hip measure as an additional guide.

Dresses 1A7, 1A404 and 1A405 on page 11 are for stout figures and come in sizes 39 to 53 bust measure, skirt length 41 inches.

IA26
IA226
$10⁹⁸
FAILLE SILK

Women's Stylish Dresses

1A419—An Exceptionally Well-made Dress of Finely Embroidered Voile, trimmed with lace-edged and hemstitched organdie collar and cuffs. The double front closing is effected with novelty buttons through the panel of plain organdie. Four tiny plaits relieve severity at the back of waist. The scalloped edges of the embroidered voile extend slightly over the organdie panel at either side of the waist front. The two-section skirt is slightly gathered beneath the soft silk girdle. White dress with maize, flesh or white girdle. *Sizes:* 32 to 46 bust measure.................... **$2.98**

1A419
$2.98
EMBROIDERED
VOILE

1A421
1A621
$5.98
LINEN

1A13
$4.98
JACQUARD
SILK

1A13—Dainty Summer Dress of Soft, Lustrous Jacquard Silk with figures in self color. The collar and chemisette are of net lace over the revers and collar of the material. Straight-edged and turn-back cuffs complete the sleeves. Black velvet belt and covered black velvet buttons trim the waist. The lower portion of the double skirt is plain while the top is gracefully gathered and finished at the bottom with three rows of cording and a slightly gathered ruffle of the material. *Colors:* Copenhagen, apple green or amethyst. *Sizes:* 32 to 46 bust measure.................... **$4.98**

1A420—Jaunty Two-piece Sport Costume of Awning Striped and Plain Colored Linon. The flare coat is caught with a patent leather belt at waist. Deep front facing of self material beneath the buttoned closing. Collar and cuff folds of striped material. Pretty patch pockets have turned-back folds of the material fastened with pearl buttons. Plain gored skirt of the striped fabric, cut with pleasing flare. Closes in front with buttons, through overlapping front seam. Color of Rose, Copenhagen or green linon, trimmed with striped material to match. *Sizes:* 32 to 46 bust. **$5.98**
1A620—Same as 1A420, but in misses' sizes... **$5.98**

Skirt lengths of Women's Dresses are 40 inches, with a deep basted hem for easy adjustment.

1A420
1A620
$5.98
SPORT
DRESS

1A421—Cleverly fashioned Dress of Fine White Linen. The sleeves, underarm portion and chemisette are of white voile with satin stripes. Square Embroidered collar and turned-back cuffs. Invisible closing in front with hooks and eyes beneath a two-toned button trimming. Smart double belt at waist and about hips is a new feature. Skirt has a well fitting yoke top and graceful flare. *Colors:* Golden brown or apple green with white striped top; white with pink striped top, or Copenhagen with Copenhagen striped top. *Sizes:* 32 to 46 bust measure... **$5.98**
1A621—Same as 1A421, but in misses' sizes.............. **$5.98**

1A423—Dainty Dress o Fine White Voile. The waist and skirt yoke are cut in one and confined by a lace bordered belt of the material. The closing is effected at one side of the front panel which is exquisitely embroidered. The deep pointed collar is trimmed with tiny pearl buttons and silk piping. The sleeves have a panel of embroidery and rows of hemstitching. They are finished with turned-back, braid trimmed cuffs which match the collar. A lace edged band of the voile is applied at knee depth, very cleverly simulating a tunic. The deep skirt hem is outlined with a row of lace insertion. *Colors:* White dress with pink, light blue or white silk braid trimming. *Sizes:* 32 to 46 bust measure. **$4.69**

1A623—The same as 1A423 but in small women's and misses' sizes...................... **$4.69**

1A425—Delightful Dress of Figured Voile artistically combined with plain colored voile in the bodice and skirt yoke. Embroidered voile collar and cuffs. Upper waist portion and sleeves of the flowered material. Beneath the gathered skirt yoke of the plain material is a deep flounce of the flowered voile finished with a shirred heading. A belt of plain voile with a loop and slashed end. *Colors:* Blue, pink or lavender combinations. *Sizes:* 32 to 46 bust.. **$2.98**

1A425
$2.98

1A424
$2.39

1A422
1A622
$2.69

1A423
1A623
$4.69

1A422—Dress of Striped Voile. White Voile is utilized for the collar, cuffs, for the snug fitting belt and for the patch pockets. A cross section of the material supplies the narrow front panel and here the closing is effected by means of pearl buttons. The skirt is cut with graceful flare, and is securely sewn to a firm inside belt. *Colors:* Green, lavender or pink stripes. *Sizes:* 32 to 46 bust measure. **$2.69**

1A622—The same as 1A422 but in small women's and misses' sizes........................ **$2.69**

1A424—A Good Looking Sport Dress of Durable White Linene. In the model shown, the collar, cuffs and patch pockets are a pleasing combination of white and colored linene, or all white. Convenient front closing through an overlapping seam. The leather belt passes through loops. The skirt is cut in novel outline, the patch pockets being applied to a simulated yoke. *Colors:* White with blue or all white. *Sizes:* 32 to 46 bust measure. **$2.39**

Simplicity—A Feature of These Three Dresses

1A427—Smartly Tailored Dress of Durable Linon Ramie. The neatly rounded collar, with its notched revers, and the pointed belt at waist are handsomely braided and embroidered. Pearl button-trimmed tabs are suspended from the belt and fasten the patch pockets, invisibly, with hooks and eyes. The plain tailored skirt is finished with an overlapping front seam. *Colors:* Tan or Copenhagen. *Sizes:* 32 to 46 bust measure............ **$3.98**

Skirt lengths of Women's Dresses are 40 inches long with a deep basted hem for easy adjustment.

1A427 $3.98 LINON RAMIE

1A426 $3.98 VOILE

1A428 $5.98 SHADOW LACE

1A426—Comfort and Charm are combined in this Cool Summer Dress of Figured Voile. The Quaker collar and double cuffs are of white organdie and colored voile picot edged. The collar is further enhanced by hemstitching. The belt and ruffle which heads the pouch pockets are of plain colored voile to match. The chemisette is of pin-tucked and hemstitched organdie. Crocheted buttons trim the front closing. Softly gathered skirt finished with three plaits. *Colors:* Copenhagen, rose or black combined with white. *Sizes:* 32 to 46 bust.......... **$3.98**

1A428—A Dainty Little Surplice Dress of Fine White Shadow Lace. It is carefully made over a foundation of firm white marquisette. It closes invisibly in back with hooks and eyes, where the soft silk girdle terminates in a loop with slashed ends. In front the lace crosses surplice fashion and is caught to the girdle with tiny plaited silk bows. Val lace completes the neck, the surplice, the cuffs and appears as a tiny ruffle above the hem of the two-section skirt. The cuffs are also trimmed with a fold of silk. *Colors:* White dress with pink, light blue or white ribbon. *Sizes:* 32 to 46 bust...... **$5.98**

1A430—Dainty Summer Dress of Embroidered Voile. The waist is made over a cool foundation of firm white net. The deep square collar is handsomely embroidered in two-toned floss, outline with fine thread lace insertion and finished with a tiny ruffle of picot-edged net. The front vestee is of plaited net, trimmed with lace insertion, hemstitching and crocheted buttons. The voile cuffs are borderd top and bottom with a row of insertion finished with a net ruffle. The skirt is slightly gathered both front and back, displays rows of insertion and elaborate panels of embroidery. At yoke depth a hemstitched plait extends across the front and back panels. The tunic effect of the skirt is accomplished through the introduction of a deep plait below the knee. *Colors:* White voile embroidered in blue and white or rose and white, or all white, trimmed with a silk girdle to match. *Sizes:* 32 to 46 bust measure...... **$6.98**

1A15—Charming Empire Model Dress of Finely Woven All Wool Serge. The vogue for metallic trimming is met in the elaborately embroidered design on the waist front and collar. Here gold threads combine with silk to deftly trace a very pretty pattern. Novelty button trimming. Pleasing length of line is achieved by the box plaited sections which appear both front and back below the deep yoke. Pointed cuffs of the material complete the sleeves. *Colors:* Navy or black. *Sizes:* 32 to 46 bust measure..................... **$7.98**
1A215—Same dress but in small women's and misses' sizes........................ **$7.98**

1A14
$2.98
Woven Check

1A429
$5.49
Pongee

1A429—Smart Looking Sport Costume of High Grade Cotton Pongee. The collar and cuffs are bordered with a band of contrasting pongee. Deep shoulder yoke at front and back extended to the hem in panel effect. Front closes invisibly beneath the loop and button trimming. Patch pockets with buttons and a fold and loops of the colored material. Pongee in two colors supplies the belt which distributes the fulness. *Colors:* Tan with rose, Copenhagen or green trimming. *Sizes:* 32 to 46 bust measure............................. **$5.49**

1A14—Dress of Black and White Woven Check. White organdie collar with thread lace edge. Under collar of black art satin with notched revers which extend to the belt. Black art satin supplies the cuffs and tabs on the patch pockets, which are also trimmed with metal buttons. Invisible closing at one side of the white organdie vestee, trimmed with metal buttons. Plain skirt made with an overlapping front seam and gracefully flared. *Sizes:* 32 to 46 bust measure. **$2.98**

1A15
1A215
$7.98
Wool Serge

1A430
$6.98
Emb. Voile

Style—Distinction—Quality
Two Dresses of Unusual Value

Skirt Lengths of Women's Dresses are 40 inches, with a deep basted hem for easy adjustment.

1A16
$15⁹⁸
Taffeta Silk With Georgette Crêpe

1A16—Charming Afternoon Dress of Soft Chiffon Taffeta and Fine Georgette Crêpe. One of the very newest models. The "throw-tie" belt is passed twice about the waist and fastened at the front. The collar is of Georgette, bound with the Taffeta. The Georgette sleeves are finished with deep-pointed cuffs of Taffeta, trimmed with covered buttons and completed with a corded edge. The front panel is of heavy Silk Crêpe in beautiful Paisley colorings. Slight gathers appear in the skirt yoke. Below this point a ruffle of the material, finished with a heading, extends from the side front seams entirely around the back. The center front panel of the skirt is plain, except for the two rows of cording which cross it. *Colors:* Bisque, Copenhagen or steel gray. *Sizes:* 32 to 46 bust measure............ **$15.98**

1A431—Dress of Finest Quality Colored Voile. The waist is cleverly fashioned on smart lines. The material is gathered at the neck and belt. It is outlined around the neck, across the shoulders and down the side openings with fine Filet pattern lace. Similar insertion trims the cuffs. The side gores of the skirt are stitched in plaits to hip depth and there released. *Colors:* Lavender, gold or Copenhagen. *Sizes:* 32 to 46 bust measure **$6.98**

1A631— Same as 1A431 but in Misses' and Small Women's sizes **$6.98**

1A431
1A631
$6⁹⁸
Colored Voile

17

Fashionable Dresses of Excellent Quality

14A432—Becoming Dress of Checked and Dotted Voile. Slightly shirred shoulder seams create fulness in the waist front. The deep collar and the cuffs of sheer organdie are edged with fine Val. The cuffs are trimmed with novelty buttons, similar to those which trim the invisible front closing. The skirt is made in the very latest vogue, with the tunic appearing on the side gores. Slight gathers extend around the skirt, beneath the black velvet belt. At yoke depth, front and back, these are confined by three rows of corded shirring. *Colors:* Copenhagen, green or gold checks each with white. *Sizes:* 32 to 46 bust.. **$4.98**

1A17—Handsomely Embroidered Dress of Soft Chiffon Taffeta. The embroidered design is in beautiful contrasting colored silks combined with gold threads. It adorns the front closing, the back of belt, and the fancy pouch pockets which trim the skirt. The sleeves are outlined with cordings of the material around the shoulder seams and above the flare cuffs. The deep collar is cut round in front but square in back and edged with plaited Val lace. The skirt falls in folds from beneath the soft belt of the material. Above the hem it is trimmed with two rows of cording. *Colors:* Sapphire blue, silver gray or sage green. *Sizes:* 32 to 46 bust measure............ **$13.98**

1A433
1A633
EMB. ORGANDIE **$6.98**

1A433—Pretty Frock of Finely Embroidered Colored Organdie. The waist is made over a lining of the material. The large collar of the embroidered organdie is outlined with a row of hemstitching. Hemstitching is again used to ornament the front closing and the ruffles which, trimmed with Val, complete the three-quarter sleeves. The "throw-tie" belt is finished with ball trimming and folds softly about the waist over the scant gathers of the double skirt. *Colors:* Flesh, light blue or white. *Sizes:* 32 to 46 bust measure.. **$6.98**

1A633—Same material and colors as 1A433 but in small women's and misses' sizes: 14 to 20 years.. **$6.98**

1A432
$4.98
VOILE

1A17
$13.98
EMB. TAFFETA SILK

1A434—Beautiful Dress of Finely Embroidered Black Voile. The gracefully rounded collar is of plain black voile, edged with thread lace in a very pretty pattern. The sleeve cuffs are of the embroidered material, plaited at the top over an undercuff of plain voile with a lace edge. The two-section skirt is gracefully gathered. Three rows of plaits extend around the skirt at yoke depth below which the embroidered voile appears. The crushed silk girdle is pleasingly completed with sash ends. *Sizes:* 32 to 46 inches bust measure. **$4.69**

Skirt Lengths of Women's Dresses are 40 inches, with a deep basted hem for easy adjustment.

1A18
1A218
$5.98
CRÊPE

!**A435**
$2.69
LINON

1A435—Serviceable Costume of Fine White Linon to be worn with or without a blouse. Box plaits at either side of the front closing extend from the shoulder to the pockets. The patch pockets, cuffs and collar are of colored linon, trimmed with white linon as shown. The belt crosses in front, a new style detail. The skirt is a smart plain tailored model, with only very slight gathers at the back. Invisible front closing at overlapping center seam. *Colors:* White with cadet blue or all white. *Sizes:* 32 to 46 bust measure **$2.69**

1A18—Charming Dress of Fine Cotton Crêpe, made on smart, plain tailored lines. Collar and belt embroidered in self-colored silk and gold threads. Invisible front closing. Cuffs and patch pockets trimmed with covered buttons. *Colors:* Pearl gray, Copenhagen or bisque. *Sizes:* 32 to 46 bust...... **$5.98**

1A218—Same material and colors as 1A18, but in small women's and misses' sizes.............**$5.98**

1A436—Exquisite Dress of All-over Embroidered Voile. The back of waist shows clusters of pin plaits. The front panel is of pin-tucked and plaited voile and trimmed with crocheted buttons. It is bordered on either side with the all-over embroidered material. The sleeves are also of the embroidered voile and finished with lace-edged cuffs of plain white voile to match the collar. Soft silk girdle at waist. Front and back panels of the lavishly embroidered voile. The side gores are made in double skirt effect, the embroidered material has an applied hem of plain white voile, which falls with grace above the plaited section of plain voile. *Colors:* White dress with white, light blue or pink girdle. *Sizes:* 32 to 46 bust measure................. **$3.98**

1A434
$4.69
BLACK EMB.VOILE

1A436
$3.98
EMB. VOILE

WE REACH YOU QUICKLY NO MATTER WHERE YOU LIVE

Stylish Dresses for the Spring and Summer

1A438
$4.98
Floral Voile

1A437
$5.98
Colored Voile

1A439
$4.98
Embroidered Voile

1A27
$7.98
Silk Poplin

Three Unusual Dresses for Women

1A401—Beautiful Afternoon Dress of Soft figured Voile, trimmed with picot edged Voile in plain color to match. Smart vestee of net trimmed with lace and finished with revers of the figured Voile and chic pearl buckle. Lace edged Organdie collar and cuffs. The deep pointed over-skirt lends long, graceful lines to the figure. *Colors:* Tan and blue, gray and lavender, or green and rose. *Sizes:* 32 to 46 inches bust measure........................ **$5.98**

1A2—Extremely Fashionable Sport Dress of Lustrous Silk Jersey. The collar, cuffs and "throw-tie" belt are of Roman Striped Silk Jersey, which also pipes the pockets and forms the deep band on the skirt. *Sizes:* 32 to 46 bust measure, *Colors:* Rose, gold, Copenhagen or emerald green.................. **$15.98**

1A202—Same style and colors as No. 1A2 but made in Misses' and Small Women's Sizes 14 to 20 years.............. **$15.98**

1A401
$5.98

1A1
1A201
$23.98

1A2
1A202
$15.98

1A1—Striking Georgette Costume for Theatre or Dinner Wear, with an elaborate braid design. It is made over a foundation of contrasting colored Seco Silk, which, in showing through the material greatly enhances its beauty. Below the elbow the sleeves are cut in points and trimmed with self-covered buttons. Contrasting colored picot edged Georgette supplies the collar and cuffs. *Sizes:* 32 to 46 bust measure. *Colors:* Peacock blue, as shown, gold, bisque or gray. **$23.98**

1A201—Same style and colors as No. 1A1 but made in Misses' and Small Women's Sizes 14 to 20 years...................... **$23.98**

Misses' and Small Women's Dresses in the Season's Latest Styles and Colors

1A604
$5.98

1A604—Delightfully Cool Dress of Figured Voile. Sheer Organdie Collar, hemstitched, embroidered and edged with Val. Val trimmed Organdie cuffs. Armholes piped with plain colored voile. Smart velvet belt. Fancy buttons trim the front closing and extend to the end of the overskirt. White lawn waist lining with firmly stitched inside belt. *Colors:* Blue and tan trimmed with blue, as illustrated; rose and gray trimmed with rose, or green and tan trimmed with green. *Sizes:* 14 to 20 years... **$5.98**

1A207
$12.98

1A207—Handsome Dress of Fine Quality Taffeta. Made alike both front and back. The elaborate embroidered design is skillfully achieved by gold and silk threads. An applied box plait extends from shoulder to hem and gives the appearance of long, graceful lines. The new style "Throw-tie" belt has ball ends. Fine white Georgette Collar. Sleeves have both flare and undercuffs, another new and pleasing detail. *Colors:* Bisque, as pictured. Copenhagen or apple green. *Sizes:* 14 to 20 years..... **$12.98**

Misses' Dresses   Exclusive in Design

1A219—Smart Dress of Figured Pongee. The deep double collar and the cuffs are an artful combination of white and colored organdie. The collar is trimmed with a silk tassel at each corner. The waist has white lawn lining. It closes invisibly in front beneath a double row of self-covered buttons. Three bands of narrow black velvet ribbon are stitched to the waist in belt effect and are also found on the lower edge of the softly gathered Tunic Skirt. *Colors:* Blue with gold dots, rose with blue, or apple green with red dots. *Sizes:* 14 to 20 years......... **$9.98**

1A635—Charming Summer Dress of Cool Marquisette in a pretty checked striped pattern. • The collar, cuffs and vestee are of fine organdie. The collar and cuffs are hemstitched and picot-edged. Ornamented with pearl buttons, the picot-edged organdie forms pointed tabs on the plaited belt of the material. Slight gathers at the belt and on the shoulder seams procure fulness for the waist. Softly gathered skirt with a plain front panel from either side of which white organdie plaits are applied and encircle the back. *Colors:* Rose and green; green and blue; or, gold and blue stripes with white stripes. *Sizes:* 14 to 20 years..... **$5.98**

1A634
$5.98
COLORED VOILE WITH MARQUISETTE

1A219
$9.98
FIGURED PONGEE

1A634—Trim-appearing Summer Dress of Colored Voile, artfully combined with fine white Marquisette. Really two dresses in one as the upper portion is entirely detachable leaving a finished dress beneath. The Marquisette supplies the under bodice, the sleeves with their lace-edged cuffs and the lace-edged collar. In front it is stitched in pin plaits where the closing is effected beneath the long-waisted panel of button-trimmed, colored voile. The upper portion of the double skirt is laid in fine plaits and falls with charming grace above the plaited underskirt. The underskirt is finished with a deep hem, above which appears a wide plait which completely encircles the skirt. *Colors:* Copenhagen, lavender or green voile with white marquisette. *Sizes:* 14 to 20 years.......... **$5.98**

1A635
$5.98
STRIPED MARQUISETTE WITH ORGANDIE

Size Scale for Misses' Dresses

14 yrs. bust 32 in. Skirt length 31 in.
16 yrs. bust 34 in. Skirt length 33 in.
18 yrs. bust 36 in. Skirt length 35 in.
20 yrs. bust 38 in. Skirt length 37 in.

All skirts made with a deep basted hem for easy adjustment.

OUR GUARANTEE IS ABSOLUTE—SATISFACTION ASSURED

23

1A221—Heavy Silk Poplin Afternoon Dress. Beautiful embroidered motifs stitched in contrasting color adorn the deep pointed collar and the smart patch pockets. The waist is made over a firm white muslin lining. The stitched belt fastens with hooks and eyes as it adjusts the fulness at waist. Covered buttons trim the invisible front closing Lower skirt portion gathered beneath a tiny fold which completes the waist. *Colors:* Tan, Copenhagen or apple green. *Sizes:* 14 to 20 years. **$6.98**

1A636—Exceptionally Good Value Embroidered Voile Dress. Deep pointed collar of the embroidered material. Narrow lace-edge overlay extending down the front in bretelle effect. Thread laces with crocheted buttons trim the front panel. Pin plaits and thread laces trim the sleeves. Softly gathered skirt is of plain and embroidered voile with three plaits below the hips and a deep plait above hem. *Colors:* White with blue, pink or white girdle. *Sizes:* 14 to 20 years. **$3.98**

1A637—Dress of Colored Voile, trimmed with wide Cluny Pattern Lace insertions A band of insertion appears in bodice effect between two deep plaits and also supplies the sleeve cuffs. Collar of plain voile edged with lace Invisible front closing trimmed with crocheted motifs Neat belt at waist. Skirt is slightly gathered, completed with a deep hem. a band of insertion and two deep plaits. *Colors:* Gold, Copenhagen or green. *Sizes:* 14 to 20 years. **$5.29**

1A220
$6.98
TUSSAH SILK

1A220—Sport Costume of Superior Quality Tussah Silk. The waist is of figured Tussah trimmed with plain material while in the skirt this condition is reversed. The cuffs, patch pockets and collar are of plain material, banded with figured goods. Stitched belt of plain Tussah. The skirt is a plain gored model, firmly stitched to the net underwaist and finished with a deep applied hem of Figured Tussah. *Colors:* Tan with Paisley colored large polka dots. *Sizes:* 14 to 20 years... **$6.98**

1A221
$6.98
SILK POPLIN

1A636
$3.98
EMBROIDERED VOILE

1A637
$5.29
COLORED VOILE

1A638—Dress of Finest Voile in a Pretty Floral Design. The waist lining is of plain white voile, edged with lace. The neat vestee is of picot-edge organdie and appears as a sort of complement to the gracefully rounded organdie collar which is trimmed with finest thread lace insertion. The belt is piped with silk in a harmonizing shade. The cuffs are trimmed with velvet buttons and silk. The yoke skirt is trimmed with dainty pouch pockets, finished with silk binding. *Colors:* Green, pink or light blue figures on white, trimmed to match. *Sizes:* 14 to 20 years.............. **$3.98**

Superior Quality Dresses for Misses and Small Women

1A222—Dress of Fine Quality Chiffon Taffeta. Fashioned in the latest mode. An embroidered design achieved by gold and silk threads is found in the waist front and on the patch pockets, collar and cuffs. The "throw-tie" belt encircles the waist twice. The invisible closing is effected at one side of the narrow panel in the waist front which is trimmed with self-covered buttons. The embroidered collar and cuffs are of fine silk pongee with picot edge. A fold of the same material completes the patch pockets. *Colors:* Navy, gold or black, with tan pongee. *Sizes:* 14 to 20 years.................. **$13.98**

1A639
$5.98
EMBROIDERED VOILE

1A638
$3.98
FLORAL VOILE

1A222
$13.98
CHIFFON TAFFETA SILK

1A639—Smartly Designed Dress of Fine White Embroidered Voile. Ideally cool and comfortable for warm weather wear. The embroidered material, cut in novel outline, edged with lace and trimmed with crocheted buttons supplies the waist front. Here the closing is visibly achieved through a hemstitched panel of the plain material. The deep collar is hemstitched plain voile. It has a deep lace edge to match the insertion and edging on the sleeves. The latest style two-section skirt is of the richly embroidered material outlined with lace insertions and completed by a deep hem. Above the hem making a pleasing finish appear two deep plaits of plain voile. *Colors:* White dress with pink, light blue or maize silk girdle. *Sizes:* 14 to 20 years. **$5.98**

Size Scale for Misses' Dresses
14 yrs., bust 32 ins., skirt length 31 ins.
16 yrs., bust 34 ins., skirt length 33 ins.
18 yrs., bust 36 ins., skirt length 35 ins.
20 yrs., bust 38 ins., skirt length 37 ins.
All skirts made with a deep basted hem for easy adjustment.

Two Dainty Voile Dresses
and
An Unusual Sport Model

1A640—Party Dress of Finely Embroidered Voile. The deep collar and bretelles are of the embroidered material edged with fine Point Lace. The waist panel front is of plain voile, stitched in plaits, outlined with lace insertion and crocheted buttons. The large "suspended" patch pockets have an embroidered motif with lace insertions and edging. In back the waist is finely plaited beneath the deep collar which extends almost to the belt. The sleeves are embroidered with large polka dots and trimmed with lace and insertion. The skirt is of the all-over embroidered material, finished with three rows of plaits. *Colors:* White with light blue, maize or white girdle. *Sizes:* 14 to 20 years..... **$8.98**

1A641—A Beautiful Embroidered Voile Afternoon Dress. The embroidery at the yoke portion is applied in tab effect. Val lace trims the neck, the deep embroidered collar and the hemstitched embroidered cuffs. The waist is made over a net foundation to which the full plaited skirt is attached. It is confined by a "throw-tie" belt of soft silk. The lower waist portion is of the elaborately embroidered voile, joined at the waist by a row of hemstitching. Plaits of different widths encircle the skirt which is a graceful side plaited model. *Colors:* White dress with light blue, pink or maize girdle. *Sizes:* 14 to 20 years...................... **$5.98**

1A640
$8.98
EMB. VOILE

1A641
$5.98
EMB. VOILE

1A223
$9.98
FAILLE SILK

1A223—New Model Sport Dress of Excellent Quality Faille Silk. Finished at the front with a double "closing," with two-toned Faille covered buttons. The cuffs are of contrasting colored Faille and finished with deep points. Deep square collar is edged with contrasting colored Faille. The smart new style "throw-tie" belt is of contrasting color and finished with knotted ends. The skirt is an extremely smart model, being completed with a deep hem of contrasting colored Faille. Firm underwaist of white muslin. *Colors:* White with navy blue or green, or tan with green. *Sizes:* 14 to 20 years......... **$9.98**

Misses' Dresses for Every Occasion

1A643—A Cool-looking Summer Dress of striped and plain colored Voile. The smooth setting collar is of fine white organdie finished with a row of hemstitching and a border of the striped material. Silk tie at neck. Plain colored voile supplies the cuffs which are trimmed with the striped fabric. The neat black silk belt at waist adjusts the fulness to the wearer's liking. The two-section skirt is of the plain colored and striped voile, finished at knee depth with a plait. *Colors:* Copenhagen or rose combinations. *Sizes:* 14 to 20 years.................. **$2.98**

1A644—Exquisite Frock of Embroidered Net over a Seco Silk Foundation. Embroidered net appears over the shoulders in bretelle effect and also supplies the upper skirt portion which is softly gathered and finished with a flounce of hemstitched plain net. The sleeves are of plain net, finished with a hemstitched ruffle and a fold of silk. The center panel of the waist is softly gathered and trimmed with narrow silk ribbon. Buttons trim the pretty silk girdle and the waist panel. *Colors:* White net, with light blue, pink or maize colored lining and trimming. *Sizes:* 14 to 20 years............................... **$7.98**

1A643
$2 <u>**98**</u>
STRIPED AND
COLORED
VOILE

1A642
$5 <u>**98**</u>
SPORT
DRESS

1A224
$7 <u>**98**</u>
TAFFETA
SILK

1A644
$7 <u>**98**</u>
EMB. NET OVER
SECO SILK

1A642—Jaunty Sport Costume of Novelty Striped Ramie Linene. The back of the coat is made with a neat slot seam from neck to hem. Novelty pouch pockets, belt, collar and stitched cuffs of the material. Pearl buttons trim the pockets and belt and form the front closing. The gracefully gathered skirt is joined to the white muslin underwaist. *Colors:* Tan with rose, blue or apple green stripes. *Sizes:* 14 to 20 years..................... **$5.98**

1A224—Pretty Afternoon Dress of Soft Chiffon Taffeta. The deep Quaker collar is finely embroidered, inset with a row of hemstitching and finished with a scalloped edge. Turned-back cuffs of embroidery complete the sleeves. The neat little patch pockets are made with a heading of the material. Shirrings form an effective belt and secure grace and fulness for the skirt. *Colors:* Navy or black. *Sizes:* 14 to 20 years..... ..... **$7.98**

NO BETTER VALUES ANYWHERE AT THE SAME PRICES

27

Misses' and Small Women's Inexpensive and Serviceable Dresses

1A645—Party Frock of Fine White Shadow Lace. Low, square neck trimmed with chiffon roses. Under-sleeves sewn on white net foundation. Shadow lace falls over the shoulders to the lace edged cuffs of the under-sleeves. Center panels of waist, front and back, slightly gathered and finished with lace ruffle. The three-section softly gathered skirt falls in folds from beneath the silk girdle. *Colors:* White with pink, light blue or white girdle. *Sizes:* 14 to 20 years........ **$3.98**

1A646
$1.49

1A225
$2.98
WOVEN CHECK

1A647
$2.59

1A645
$3.98
SHADOW LACE

1A646—Two-Piece Sport Costume of White Tub Gabardine which may be worn with or without a blouse. The collar, cuffs, patch pockets and belt ends are of blue and white or rose and white linene. The belt passes through loops at waist and fastens "throw-tie" in front. The skirt is a plain tailored model and closes invisibly with hooks and eyes beneath an overlapping front seam. *Colors:* as described. *Sizes:* 14 to 20 years............... **$1.49**

1A225—Trim Appearing Dress of Woven Check, trimmed with pipings of red sateen and novelty bone buttons. The pipings are extended down the front in novel outline and finish the convenient patch pockets. It also outlines the circular collar and the pointed cuffs of the long sleeves. Small loops of soutache braid finished with fancy ends complete the neck. The plain skirt is cut with pleasing flare lines. *Colors:* as described. *Sizes:* 14 to 20 years.................. **$2.98**

1A647—Serviceable Dress of White Linene. Pleasing contrast is offered in the blue or red linene which serves as a trimming on the square collar and cuffs. Cross-stitch embroidery trims the belt, while floss covered balls in two tones appear at the neck and on the points of the novelly shaped sleeves. Three deep plaits stitched from shoulder seams to hip depth in front, contribute desirable grace to the skirt. In back the dress is made with plaits which extend from yoke to belt. Below the button-trimmed belt side plaits fall gracefully to the hem. *Colors:* As described. *Sizes:* 14 to 20 years.......... **$2.59**

Misses' Dresses for Every Day Wear

1A648—Neatly Made Dress of Fine French Linon. The closing is effected with hooks and eyes beneath the narrow front panel which is outlined with pretty square pearl buttons. Similar buttons trim the deep pointed patch pockets. The cuffs are of hemstitched picot-edged white organdie. The same material also supplies the collar, which is finished with a neat bow of the linon. Patent leather belt at waist, trimmed with white kid and metal buckles, passes through loops and so distributes the fulness. *Colors:* Rose, tan or Copenhagen. *Sizes:* 14 to 20 years. **$4.49**

See Size Scale on Page 23

1A650—A Dress Frock of Elaborately Embroidered Voile, inset with thread lace insertions and fine pin tucks. The back of waist has two clusters of pin tucks which extend from the neck to the belt. Embroidered voile supplies the waist front, which is inset with a panel of the material outlined with thread lace edging and insertion. The sleeves show clusters of pin tucks and thread lace cuffs. The upper portion of the double skirt is made with a panel of the embroidered voile combined with insertion. A band of the embroidered material is outlined with rows of pin tucking and insertion and finished with a lace edge. The lower skirt portion is entirely of the embroidered voile, finished with a scalloped edge. *Colors:* White dress with pink, light blue or white girdle. *Sizes:* 14 to 20 years. **$2.98**

1A651—A Good Serviceable Dress of Chambray and Checked Gingham. Pipings of Gingham trim the belt, cuffs and patch pockets. Checked gingham collar. Hand-smocking at either side of front closing, which is effected with braid loops and pearl buttons. The skirt is of the checked gingham, finished with a chambray hem. Neat band at waist. Invisible side closing. *Colors:* Tan, green or blue, trimmed with plain colored chambray to match. *Sizes:* 14 to 20 years. **$2.59**

1A650
$2.98
EMBROIDERED VOILE

1A649
$2.29
STRIPED VOILE

1A649—Dress of Striped Voile with the waist and skirt yoke cut in one. Soft satin girdle at waist depth adjusts the fulness, and fastens the new "throw-tie" way or in a bow, as preferred. Below the yoke the material is cut crosswise of the goods and forms a deep ruffle with a corded edge. Plain white voile, finished with lace edged, hemstitched cuffs of the material. Deep square collar of white organdie edged with thread lace and neatly hemstitched. *Colors:* Rose, green or blue stripes on white ground. *Sizes:* 14 to 20 years. **$2.29**

1A648
$4.49
LINON

1A651
$2.59
CHAMBRAY WITH GINGHAM

SATISFACTION GUARANTEED OR YOUR MONEY REFUNDED

29

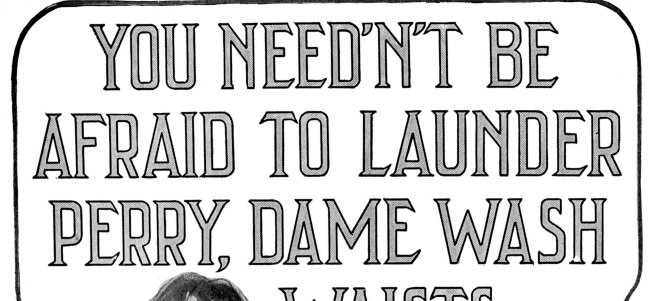

YOU NEED'N'T BE AFRAID TO LAUNDER PERRY, DAME WASH WAISTS

EVERY WAIST IS MOST CAREFULLY MADE

EVERY SEAM IS SECURELY SEWN

THE MATERIALS ARE DURABLE

THE COLORS WILL NOT RUN

LATEST STYLE WAISTS WITH THE PERRY-DAME GUARANTEE

9A1
$1.25

ALL OVER EMB. ORGANDIE

Elegant Waist of All Over Embroidered Organdie

9A1—A Beautiful Dressy Waist of Finest All Over Embroidered Organdie. The deep square collar is neatly hem stitched all around and finished with a deep Val lace edge. It is of sheer organdie and the embroidered material in showing through the collar produces a very dainty effect. The shoulder seams are also prettily hemstitched and here slight gathers are introduced to insure the proper degree of fulness for the waist front. The closing is effected at the center front with a single row of fine pearl buttons. The cuff of plain organdie is trimmed with a turned-back plain organdie fold finished with a row of hemstitching at the top and bottom. *Colors:* White only. *Sizes:* 32 to 46 bust measure. In this waist we offer you a Special Perry-Dame value—an excellent sample of the superiority of our merchandise.............................. **$1.25**

Women's Smart Waists

9A5—Women's and Misses' Sport Middy of White Galatea. Contrasting colored Ramie Linene supplies the collar, cuffs and belt and combined with pearl buttons finishes the patch pockets. Hand smocking at either side of front below the yoke, and on the pockets. Hand sprigging on the deep collar and cuffs. *Colors:* White with Copenhagen or rose. *Sizes:* 32 to 46 bust and 14 to 20 years.. **$1.69**

9A2—Tailored Blouse of Fine White Linene, handsomely embroidered in solid and eyelet design. Front plaits stitched to yoke depth. The embroidery appears upon the novelly shaped collar, which terminates in neat revers. It also trims the waist front at either side of the closing which is effected with small pearl buttons. *Sizes:* 32 to 46 bust.. **$1.00**

9A3—Blouse of Fine Ecru Net. Made over a net foundation. The panel is an artful combination of pin-plaited net set between rows of embroidered net finished on either side with fine hemstitching. Deep square collar of plain and embroidered net hemstitched and edged with net ruffle. Hemstitched and embroidered cuffs finished with a ruffle. Ecru only. *Sizes:* 32 to 46 bust.........**$2.98**

NET WITH EMBROIDERY

9A5
$1.69
HAND EMB.
GALATEA

9A3
$2.98

9A2
$1.00
EMB. LINENE

9A4—Well-made Waist of Soft Lustrous Jap Silk. The embroidered motif whch ornaments the front is in two-toned silk to match the piping, which appears all around the collar. The collar is the most charming feature of the waist; it is gracefully rounded in back and extends down the front almost to the belt. Turned-back cuffs piped in contrasting color. Front closing with pearl buttons. *Colors:* All white or white with rose or maize piping. *Sizes:* 32 to 46 bust measure. A waist of unusual beauty and design which will launder well and wear to your entire satisfaction........................ **$2.25**

9A4
$2.25
EMB. JAP SILK

9A10—Waist of Soft Lustrous Seco Silk, neatly embroidered in self color in a dot and flower spray pattern. The square collar is edged with Filet pattern lace. Cuffs of the material. *Colors:* White, rose or maize. *Sizes:* 32 to 46 bust. **$1.69**

9A11—Women's and Misses' Sport Middy of Novelty Crash. Pearl buttons and braid loops trim the collar and patch pockets, of natural colored crash. Crash belt adjusts the fulness and fastens at one side in a "throw-tie." *Colors:* Rose, blue or green stripes on tan back ground. *Sizes:* 32 to 44 bust. Misses' sizes 14 to 20 years.............................. **$1.69**

9A8—Carefully Made Crêpe de Chine Waist. The collar and the panels at either side of the front closing are of fine filet pattern lace. Cuffs of crêpe de chine complete the sleeves. *Colors:* Flesh, maize or white. *Sizes:* 32 to 46 bust measure.......... **$2.49**

Tub Silk
9A10
$1.69

Silk Crepe de Chine
9A8
$2.49

Novelty Crash
9A11
$1.69

Voile
9A9
$1.25

9A9—A Charming Waist of Fine White Voile. The front is prettily trimmed with finely embroidered lace-edged frills. The shoulder seams and cuffs are outlined with hemstitching. The deep square collar is of fine voile edged with Val. *Sizes:* 32 to 46 bust measure........ **$1.25**

9A6—Beautifully Embroidered Voile Waist. The embroidery, inset with hemstitching, finishes the collar and the plaited and embroidered waterfall revers in the waist front. Hemstitched shoulder seams. *Colors:* White with rose or blue embroidery. *Sizes:* 32 to 46 inches bust measure................ **.89**

9A7—Chic Blouse of Finest Quality White Organdie. Pin tucks and fine plaits appear entirely across the front. Double closing with fine pearl buttons outlined with ribbon run tie and hemstitching. Bands of embroidered organdie trim the collar and hemstitched cuffs, fastened with a ribbon bow. Pin tucks and plaits trim the back. *Colors:* White with black ribbon. *Sizes:* 32 to 46 bust. **$1.98**

Voile
9A6
89¢

Organdie
9A7
$1.98

Three Stylish Waists and an Exceptionally Beautiful Middy

Habutai 9A13 $3.98

Women's and Misses' Middy

9A15 — Exceptionally Beautiful Hand Smocked Sport Middy of finest quality Mercerized Poplin. The novelly cut collar, with its pretty double points at front, and the cuffs are of contrasting colored poplin, trimmed with fancy pearl buttons. Bands of the colored poplin trimmed with buttons complete the smart patch pockets. Fine hand-made silk smocking in white ornaments the front and also beautiful smart back in panel effect. New model "throw-tie" belt with tassel ends. *Colors:* White with rose, gold or Copenhagen. *Sizes:* 32 to 44 bust. Also 14 to 20 years....................... **$4.98**

Hand Smocked Mercerized Poplin 9A15 $4.98

Net 9A14 $2.69

Voile 9A12 $1.29

9A12 — Delightful Waist of Fine Quality White Voile. Made in the latest vogue. The shoulder seams and the cuffs, with their turned-back fold of the material show rows of hemstitching. The deep handsome collar is of beautiful sheer white organdie with a scalloped edge and fine flowers embroidered in colors. It is a special feature of this particularly dainty waist. *Colors:* White waist embroidered with Hague blue and rose colored silk in a dainty floral pattern. *Sizes:* 32 to 46 bust measure. **$1.29**

9A13 — Neatly Tailored Waist of Satin Striped Habutai Silk. Soft and fine as Pussy Willow. The collar and turned-back cuffs are of plain white Habutai faced with Jap silk. Slight gathers on the shoulder seams relieve all tendency toward plainness. Two very beautiful large pearl buttons form the closing. *Colors:* White with navy, Nile green or lavender stripes. *Sizes:* 32 to 46 bust measure. A smart plain model, one of the season's latest designs.................... **$3.98**

9A14 — Cream Colored Net Waist made over a foundation of plain net. The collar is of pin-pleated net outlined with hemstitching and finished with a narrow net ruffle. The front of waist displays pin-tucked revers, edged all around with a net ruffle and is trimmed with lace motifs and hemstitching. Front closing with novelty buttons. Cream only. *Sizes:* 32 to 46 bust measure. A beautiful dress model made in the latest mode...................................... **$2.69**

Stylishly Becoming Waists and Middies

9A20
$1.98
ETAMINE CLOTH

9A17
98¢
VOILE

9A20—Women's and Misses' Fashionable Sport Coat of Finely Woven Etamine Cloth. Pleasing contrast is seen in the collar, cuffs, belt and patch pocket trimming of fine white mercerized poplin. Large pearl buttons form the closing while smaller sized buttons trim the collar. The "throw-tie" belt is completed with tassels. *Colors:* Rose, Copenhagen or orchid. *Sizes:* 32 to 44 bust and 14 to 20 years. . **$1.98**

9A16—Handsome, New Style Waist of Fine Jacquard Tub Silk, easily laundered. The gracefully rounded, double collar of sheer organdie is stitched in color to contrast with the stripes of the dainty material. Turned-back organdie cuffs with colored picot edge complete the sleeves. *Colors:* Rose and blue, rose and green, green and lavender stripes. *Sizes:* 32 to 46 bust measure. A very special offering........ **$1.49**

JACQUARD TUB SILK
9A16
$1.49

9A17—Fine White Voile Waist. It is lavishly trimmed with Filet pattern lace and panels of fine embroidery in a dainty flower design. The deep square organdie collar and the waist front are richly trimmed with the lace. Hemstitching outlines the shoulder seams and the cuffs. Pin plaits trim the back of waist. *Sizes:* 32 to 46 bust measure. The quality of the materials and excellence of its manufacture make this a most unusual waist......... **.98**

9A19
$1.00
GALATEA

9A18—Neatly Made Waist of Fine Silk Crêpe de Chine, daintily trimmed with tiny lace revers and vestee. The little breast pockets are also of the Filet pattern lace. *Colors:* White or flesh. *Sizes:* 32 to 46 bust measure. An extremely pretty waist suitable for wear on dress occasions......... **$2.25**

SILK CREPE DE CHINE
9A18
$2.25

Women's and Misses' Middy
9A19—Another Pretty Galatea Middy is here pictured. The collar, cuffs, belt and patch pocket trimming are of plain colored Ramie Linene in a contrasting shade. Made with a shoulder yoke and front lacing. The belt passes through loops at waist and adjusts the fulness. *Colors:* All white or white trimmed with rose or Copenhagen. *Sizes:* 32 to 44 bust measure. Misses' sizes 14 to 20 years............ **$1.00**

Three Beautiful Waists and a Poplin Middy

9A23 $2⁴⁹ HAND EMB VOILE

9A23—Beautifully Hand Embroidered Waist of Fine White Voile. The back of the collar is cut in scalloped outline, ornamented with the embroidered design and edged with fine Val lace. Embroidery is again seen on the front ends of the collar and on the lace-edged frill at either side of the hemstitched front closing. The cuffs are embroidered to match, outlined with hemstitching and finished with a lace-edged flare cuff. *Colors:* White waist with white and blue embroidery. *Sizes: 32 to 46 bust measure.* **$2.49**

9A22 $1²⁹ VOILE

9A24 $2¹⁹ STRIPED POPLIN

Women's and Misses' Sport Coat

9A24—Stylish Middy Coat of Fine Poplin effectively trimmed with white galatea. The galatea furnishes the belt which crosses in front, one of the latest style features this Spring. Combined with the material it supplies the deep square collar, the cuffs and the patch pockets. A cross section of the material simulates a panel front and here the closing is accomplished with fine pearl buttons. *Colors:* Tan and rose, blue and gold or white and lilac. *Sizes:* 32 to 46 bust measure.. **$2.19**

9A22—Neat Waist of Colored Voile. Slight gathers along the shoulder seams and box plaits at either side of the front relieve all tendency toward severity. The collar and cuffs are of plain white organdie finished with a picot-edged ruffle of the colored material. *Colors:* Rose or blue. *Sizes: 32 to 46 bust measure.....* **$1.29**

9A21—A Handsome Dress Waist of All Over Embroidered French Voile. The embroidery is in an elaborate flower and dotted pattern. The deep square collar terminates in tiny revers edged with fine Point de Paris Pattern Lace. Similar lace completes the cuffs, which are outlined with a row of hemstitching. Fine hemstitching also defines the armholes and the shoulder seams. Panels of the lace bordered by fine plaits make a very effective and pretty waist front. White only. *Sizes:* 32 to 46 bust measure..... **$2.49**

9A21 $2⁴⁹ ALL OVER EMB. FRENCH VOILE

An Attractive Middy and Waists of Unusual Value

9A28
98¢

9A25—Neatly Tailored Waist of Fine Habutai Silk. The cuffs, the front vestee and the collar are of plain white Habutai. The collar is cut square in back and finished with a hemstitched hem. *Colors:* Black and white or blue and white stripes on white ground. *Sizes:* 32 to 46 bust measure........................**$2.25**

9A26—Thoroughly Up-to-date Waist of Fine Paisley Voile with a double organdie collar and cuffs. Hemstitched collar and cuffs. Slight gathers along the shoulder seams give pleasing fulness to the waist front. The slip knot tie is of the Paisley voile, finished with plain colored ends to match the collar and cuffs. *Colors:* Paisley colored voile with rose or blue trimming. *Sizes:* 32 to 46 bust measure.....................................**$1.25**

9A28—Serviceable Sport Middy of Durable White Lonsdale Jean. The collar and cuffs of the three-quarter sleeves are of contrasting colored linene. Linene supplies the trimming on the pointed patch pockets. The back of the middy is plain, the fulness being distributed to the wearer's liking by aid of the neatly stitched belt which passes through loops made in the box plaits at either side of the front closing. *Sizes:* 32 to 44 bust measure, 14 to 20 years for misses and small women. *Colors:* All white, or white trimmed with Copenhagen or rose.....................................**.98**

9A25
$2 25
HABUTAI SILK

9A27—Dainty Waist of Fine White French Voile. The collar and revers are cut in novel outline and pleasingly trimmed with an embroidery design and fine Point de Paris pattern lace. The pointed sections are finished with a neat picot edge. The shoulder seams and armholes are defined by a row of hemstitching. Hemstitching also outlines the cuffs which are of voile and lace insertion, finished with a picot-edged ruffle. *Sizes:* 32 to 46 bust............ **$2.25**

9A27
$2 25
FRENCH VOILE

9A26
$1 25
PAISLEY VOILE

9A31—An Exquisitely Embroidered Dress Waist of Fine White Organdie. The waist front is a beautiful combination of the finely embroidered material bordered by fine box plaits. The deep collar is square in back and finished with a row of hemstitching and a deep Val edge. The shoulder seams and the cuffs with their turned back fold of organdie are neatly hemstitched. *Sizes:* 32 to 46 bust measure. **$1.25**

Galatea
9A34
$1.29

Emb.
Organdie
9A31
$1.25

Perry-Dame Price Saving Opportunities

9A32—Tailored Waist of Striped Madras, an excellent wearing material. Carefully made in every detail. The neat breast pockets are finished with buttoned tabs. Mannish collar with small revers. Turned-back cuffs of the material complete the sleeves. Finished with tie strings for securing the blouse in proper position. *Colors:* Blue or rose stripes on white ground. *Sizes:* 32 to 46 bust measure....... **$1.25**

9A33—Soft Chiffon Taffeta Blouse with fine pin tucks made in plaid effect across the entire front. The back of the blouse is plain. Slight gathers on the shoulder seams. The gracefully rounded collar has small revers. Neat turned-back pointed cuffs complete the sleeves. *Colors:* Navy blue or black. *Sizes:* 32 to 44 bust measure............... **$3.49**

9A34—Smart Appearing Sport Middy Coat of Fine White Galatea. The collar, cuffs, belt and patch pockets are very unusual in style and effectively trimmed with contrasting colored awning striped material. The belt is made in the latest vogue and crosses in front, fastening with fine buttons to the patch pockets. Large pearl buttons form the closing. *Colors:* White Middy trimmed with rose and white or blue and white striped material. *Sizes:* 32 to 44 bust measure........................ **$1.29**

9A30—Dainty Waist of Fine White Embroidered Voile. The square collar and the cuffs are edged with fine Val. Hemstitching outlines the cuffs, armholes and shoulder seams. It also simulates a yoke in back, where slight gathers create pleasing fulness. Finely embroidered Voile front. Hemstitched front closing effected with pearl buttons. *Sizes:* 32 to 46 bust. **$1.79**

9A32
$1.25

Novelty
Voile
9A29
98¢

9A29—Exceptionally good Value is offered you in this waist of Novelty Voile, with large Paisley colored Polka dots interspersed with smaller dots in all-over effect. The collar and cuffs are of hemstitched Organdie. The revers and back of collar are stitched in a pretty embroidered floral pattern. Black ribbon slip-knot tie. *Colors:* Flesh or white background with Paisley dots. *Sizes:* 32 to 46 bust measure................. **.98**

Emb.
Voile
9A30
$1.79

9A33
Taffeta Silk $3.49

9A39
$1.98

9A38
$3.29

9A37
$3.98
SILK FINISHED GROS-GRAIN

9A44
$3.98
SILK CRÊPE DE CHINE →

9A40
$2.49

9A41
$1.25

9A43
$4.98
SILK GEORGETTE CRÊPE

9A42
$2.49

FOR DESCRIPTIONS OF THESE WAISTS SEE FACING PAGE

Fashionable Waists

9A45
$1.19

9A47
$4.49

9A46
$1.29

9A45—Extremely Fashionable Waist of Plaid and Polka-dotted Voile. It has a double collar and cuffs of picot-edged organdie, one of which matches the predominating color in the body of the waist while the other is of white. Necessary fulness is procured by the introduction of slight gathers along the shoulder seams. *Colors:* Rose, maize or Copenhagen blue plaid and dots on a white ground. *Sizes:* 32 to 46 inches bust measure. A well made waist which will find favor with everyone.. **$1.19**

9A49
$6.98
SILK
GEORG-
ETTE
CRÊPE

9A48
$3.98

9A46—Beautiful Paisley Pattern Voile Waist. The Paisley revival has met with universal approval. This waist is decidedly up to date in every detail. The collar is cut in naval outline and ornamented with hemstitching. The scalloped revers are finely embroidered. *Sizes:* 32 to 46 inches bust measure. A serviceable waist which will harmonize with any color skirt............ **$1.29**

9A49—Exquisitely Dainty Waist of Fine Georgette Crêpe. The front is elaborately embroidered with beads, gold threads and rich toned silks to match the collar and cuffs. These are of fine quality picot-edged Taffeta. Fine hemstitching outlines the armholes, shoulder seams and front panel where the waist fastens with a double row of buttonholes and silk-covered buttons. This double closing is distinctly new. *Colors:* Biscuit and Purple, Burgundy and Gold, White and Flesh, Flesh and Light Blue. *Sizes:* 32 to 46 inches bust measure. This waist is a beauty. Wonderfully attractive in design and of splendid material and workmanship... **$6.98**

9A48—Remarkably Beautiful Waist of Silk Lace and Fine Net. The delicate Bisque shade of the lace is further enhanced by the Flesh-toned Chiffon which trims the waist front, the collar and the cuffs. A decidedly new note in lace waists is seen on the waist front and on the collar, where gold thread traces a finely embroidered design and supplies two small tassels. *Sizes:* 32 to 46 inches bust measure. A dainty waist especially adapted for theatre and dinner wear.,.......... **$3.98**

9A47—Chic Waist of Fine Quality Flesh or White Crêpe de Chine. A new and unusually attractive model. The deep square back collar, with its embroidered corners and lace edge, trims both the front and back of the waist and is a fashionable new feature this season. Pin tucks and plaits at either side of the front relieve any tendency toward severity. Hemstitching simulates cuffs on the sleeves. *Sizes:* 32 to 46 inches bust measure...... **$4.49**

Newest Style Skirts of Quality for All Occasions

9A52
$3⁹⁸
FLORAL CHIFFON & SHADOW LACE

9A51
$2²⁵
EMB. VOILE

5A2
5A52
$7⁹⁸
VELOUR PLAID

5A3
$3⁹⁸
POPLIN

Two Charming Waists

9A51—Handsomely Embroidered White Voile Waist. Trimmed with Point de Paris Pattern lace and insertion. Panels of the insertion appear at either side of the front closing, which is accomplished by means of fancy pearl buttons. The deep collar of the embroidered voile is edged with lace and has insertions at either side. The cuffs are hemstitched and have turned-back folds of the voile, edged with lace. Sizes: 32 to 46 bust measure... **$2.25**

9A52—Delicately Beautiful Waist. Cream Colored Silk Shadow Lace combined with Silk Flowered Chiffon with dainty flowers in pastel shades. Hemstitching outlines the collar, cuffs and the seams where chiffon and lace join. Collar of silk lace with band of flowered chiffon across back. Silk lace revers. Silk lace panel in waist front where the invisible closing is effected. The waist lining is of silk chiffon. Sizes: 32 to 46 bust. **$3.98**

5A2—An Extremely Up-to-date Skirt of Velour Plaid. Trimmed with deep fringe—one of Fashion's latest fancies. Slight shirrings and pin plaits relieve all tendency toward severity. The long pointed tabs of the material which appear at either side hang loosely from the belt and are fitted with small patch pockets and button-trimmed flap. Here the vogue for deep fringe trimming is pleasingly displayed. The deep belt of the material is fastened at the front with hooks and eyes beneath two large novelty buttons which supply the trimming. Sizes: 22 to 30 inches waist. Lengths: 36 to 43 inches. Colors: Black and white plaid with blue overplaid... **$7.98**

5A52—The same style and material but in small women's and misses' sizes: 22 to 28 inches waist. Lengths: 33 to 35 inches........ **$7.98**

5A3—Cleverly Designed Skirt of Wool Poplin cut on mannish lines. Very slight gathers beneath the belt at back prevent all tendency toward dragging across the hips. The front is plain and slashed pockets trimmed with pearl buttons appear at each side. Colors: Black or navy blue. Sizes: 22 to 30 inches waist. Lengths: 36 to 43 inches.. **$3.98**

Stylish Skirts of Rich Materials

5A5—Stylish Sport Skirt of Beautiful Soft Velvet Corduroy. The front is plain, while the back is slightly gathered to gain an easy fit. The extra large patch pockets are an extremely fashionable feature. They are finished with deep pointed tabs of the material and trimmed with buttons. The neat belt is detachable and trimmed with pearl buttons. *Colors:* Rose, Copenhagen, white or gold. *Sizes:* 22 to 30 waist. Lengths: 36 to 43 inches........ **$4.39**

5A55—Same style and colors as No. 5A5, but made in Misses' and Small Women's Sizes. Waist: 22 to 28 inches. Lengths: 33 to 35 inches........ **$4.39**

Samples of Perry-Dame Skirt Materials will be sent you gladly, FREE.

5A5
5A55
$4.39
VELVET CORDUROY

5A4
$5.25
PANAMA POPLIN

5A4—High Grade Tailoring and Superior Quality Wool Panama Poplin combine to make this skirt one of our best offerings. The belt is cut in yoke effect, trimmed with bone buttons and rows of stitching to simulate buttonholes. At either side of the front three side plaits are stitched to below the yoke and there released. The centre panel of the back has slight gathers beneath the belt and the closing is effected at one side of this panel. *Colors:* Black or navy. *Sizes:* 22 to 30 waist. Lengths: 36 to 43 inches......... **$5.25**

5A6—Smart, Plain Tailored Skirt of Serviceable Serge. The overlapping seam at the front, beneath which the closing is effected, is trimmed at the bottom with bone buttons. The deep patch pockets are elaborately embroidered with silk braid and thread. Stitched belt at waist has slight shirrings at the back which insure the fit. *Colors:* Black or blue. *Sizes:* 22 to 30 waist. Lengths: 36 to 43 inches. A serviceable skirt of finely woven wool serge with a small percentage of cotton to increase its durability.... **$2.98**

5A6
$2.98
SERGE

Women's Skirts for All Occasions

5A10—Beautiful Dress Skirt of Finely Woven French Voile. Carefully tailored throughout and bound in every seam. The new style pendant patch pockets and the yoke belt in front are handsomely embroidered with black silk threads. The front of the skirt forms a panel while the side gores are laid in graceful side plaits. Beneath the belt in back the material is slightly shirred to procure requisite fulness and graceful lines. Side front closing. *Color:* Black only. *Sizes:* 22 to 30 inches waist. Lengths: 36 to 43 inches... **$4.69**

5A7
$4.98
ALL WOOL SERGE

5A8
5A53
$3.49
STRIPED BEACH CLOTH

5A9
$3.98
SERGE

5A10
$4.69
VOILE

5A7—Up-to-date Skirt of Fine All Wool Serge. The vogue for metallic trimming is seen on the belt and on the new style plaited Patch Pocket where silk and silver threads are worked into an elaborate embroidered design. The overlapping front seam is trimmed at the bottom with clusters of bone buttons, similar to those which trim the belt in back. The slightly shirred back produces a perfect fitting skirt. Invisible side closing. *Colors:* Black or navy. *Sizes:* 22 to 30 waist. Lengths: 36 to 43 inches... **$4.98**

5A8—A Well Tailored Skirt of Wear Resisting Black and White Striped Beach Cloth. An Excellent Summer material, as it sheds the dust very readily and is cool and comfortable. Beneath the belt at back slight gathers insure perfect fit. Bone buttons trim the pendant patch pockets and fasten the belt. The front panel is stitched to knee depth and then released, it falls in inverted plaits to the hem. Side closing. *Sizes:* 22 to 30 waist. Lengths: 36 to 43 inches... **$3.49**

5A53—Same style and colors as No. 5A8, but made in Misses' and Small Women's Sizes: Waist: 22 to 28. Lengths: 33 to 35 inches... **$3.49**

5A9—Serviceable Skirt of Good Grade Serge, well made and neatly finished throughout. Pin tucks in back stitched to hip depth insure a smooth fit. The belt is trimmed with covered buttons in back. At the front it is cut in novel outline, extended down the side front seams in yoke effect and trimmed with covered buttons. The side gores are stitched to below the hips and then released to fall in side plaits to the hem. *Colors:* Black or navy. *Sizes:* 22 to 30 waist. Lengths: 36 to 43 inches... **$3.98**

Samples of Perry-Dame Skirt materials will be sent you gladly. FREE.

Perry-Dame Tailored Skirts

5A12—Delightfully Cool Summer Skirt of Lustrous Mohair. Graceful side plaits fall from below the pendant patch pockets, with their bone button trimming. The skirt is plain in back. Sufficient flare in cutting gives pleasing grace and becoming lines. Side closing. *Sizes:* 22 to 30 inches waist measure. Length: 36 to 43 inches. *Colors:* Black or navy..........**$3.98**

5A11
$3.98
Plaid Serge

5A11—Gracefully Flared Skirt of Plaid Serge. Slightly gathered at the back beneath the belt. The front closing is accomplished by bone buttons. The novelly shaped patch pockets have a button-trimmed flap. *Sizes:* 22 to 30 inches waist measure. Lengths: 36 to 43 inches. *Colors:* Blue and white or black and white plaid......**$3.98**

5A12
$3.98
Lustrous Mohair

5A13
5A51
$3.98
Wool Serge

5A14
$4.69
Wool Poplin

5A13—Beautiful Skirt of Fine All Wool Serge. Carefully tailored throughout. Slight gathers beneath the belt at back. Smart patch pockets with a button-trimmed band of the material. Side closing. *Colors:* White, navy or black. *Sizes:* 22 to 30 inches waist measure. Lengths: 36 to 43 inches........**$3.98**
5A51—Same as 5A13 but in misses' sizes: 22 to 28 waist. Lengths: 33 to 35 inches....**$3.98**

5A14—Smartly Designed Skirt of High Grade All Wool Poplin. The shallow yoke at the back is finished in front in a deep point. Below the yoke, the side plaits are trimmed with square poplin covered buttons and stitched to hip depth. *Colors:* Black or navy. *Sizes:* 22 to 30 inches waist measure. Lengths: 36 to 43 inches..........**$4.69**

Stylish—Becoming—Comfortable
These Two Skirts
Are Remarkable Values

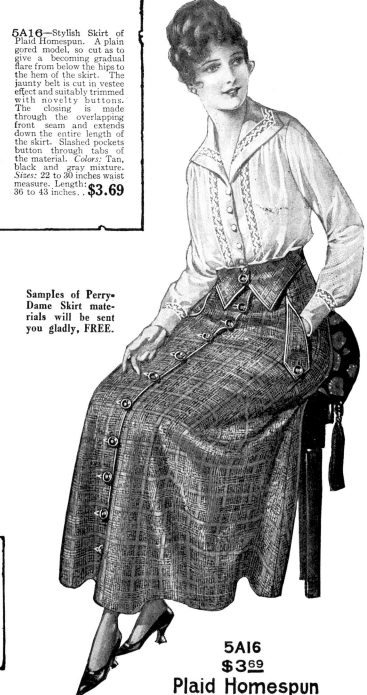

5A16—Stylish Skirt of Plaid Homespun. A plain gored model, so cut as to give a becoming gradual flare from below the hips to the hem of the skirt. The jaunty belt is cut in vestee effect and suitably trimmed with novelty buttons. The closing is made through the overlapping front seam and extends down the entire length of the skirt. Slashed pockets button through tabs of the material. *Colors:* Tan, black and gray mixture. *Sizes:* 22 to 30 inches waist measure. Length: 36 to 43 inches.. **$3.69**

Samples of Perry-Dame Skirt materials will be sent you gladly, FREE.

5A15
$6⁹⁸
Wool Poplin

5A15—Gracefully Side-plaited Skirt of Superior Quality All Wool Poplin. The plaits at the center front are so turned as to form a long straight panel line. The sides and back are beautifully plaited all around. The deep, smooth setting girdle is elaborately embroidered with silk and gold threads in front and fastens at the back with a double button and buttonhole closing. *Colors:* Black, navy or gold. *Sizes:* 22 to 30 inches waist measure. Lengths: 36 to 43 inches. This charming model is one of the handsomest dress skirts shown this season **$6.98**

5A16
$3⁶⁹
Plaid Homespun

Four Very Smart Skirts

5A17—New Model Skirt of Serviceable All Wool Poplin of very fine quality. An overlapping seam defines the buttoned front closing. Box-plaited heading of the material confined at the hips by a button-trimmed band, below which box plaits fall in graceful folds. Panel back stitched to hips and then released. *Colors:* Black or navy blue. *Sizes:* 22 to 30 waist. Lengths: 36 to 43 inches. **$5.98**

5A20—Fashionable Skirt of Superior Quality All Wool Serge. Trimly tailored and neatly finished in every seam. Serge-covered buttons trim the front, which is cut on unusual lines and stitched to simulate slashed pockets. The plaits are stitched to below the hips and then being released they give grace and fulness to the lower skirt portion. *Colors:* Black or navy. *Sizes:* 22 to 30 waist. Lengths: 36 to 43 inches..... **$4.98**

5A18
$3.39
SERGE

5A19
$3.29
SCOTCH TWEED

5A17
$5.98
WOOL POPLIN

Samples of Perry-Dame skirt materials will be sent you gladly, FREE.

5A18—A Well-setting Skirt of Good Grade, Wear-resisting Wool and Cotton Serge. Neatly finished throughout. Slashed pockets, below which the serge is side plaited to secure pleasing breadth for the lower portion of the skirt. Bone buttons trim the front panel. The stitched belt at waist extends from the side front seams to the back. There it is fastened with a button above the double row of shirring. *Colors:* Black or navy. *Sizes:* 22 to 30 waist. Lengths: 36 to 43 inches. **$3.39**

5A19—Utility Skirt of Fine Scotch Tweed. The smart slashed pockets are made with two deep button-trimmed flaps of the Tweed. The overlapping front seam defines the buttoned closing in front. Graceful flare is secured in cutting for this smart plain tailored model—ideal for sport wear. *Colors:* Brown Tweed mixture. *Sizes:* 22 to 30 waist. Lengths: 36 to 43 inches.. **$3.29**

5A20
$4.98
WOOL SERGE

Newest Spring and Summer Skirts for Women

5A23—Sport Skirt of Black, White and Gold Colored Plaid Mixture. Made with the new style "throw-tie" belt at waist. Small buttons trim the envelope patch pocket at one side and form the side front closing at the left. The skirt is plain gored in front, while slight gathers beneath the belt procure requisite flare for the back. *Sizes:* Waist: 22 to 30 inches. Lengths: 36 to 43 inches.... **$4.25**

5A49—Same style and colors as No. 5A23, but made in Misses' and Small Women's Sizes: Waist: 22 to 28 inches. Lengths: 33 to 35 inches.................. **$4.25**

5A21
5A48
$6⁹⁸
TAFFETA
SILK

Samples of Perry-Dame skirt materials will be sent you gladly, FREE.

5A23
5A49
$4²⁵
PLAID
MIXTURE

A521—Beautiful Dress Skirt of Soft Black Taffeta Silk. Shirred on an elastic band at waist. The shirrings continue to hip depth to acquire necessary grace and fulness. The detachable "Chatelaine" Pocket of Taffeta Silk is suspended from the belt, lined throughout and finished at the bottom with rows of shirring and a pretty silk tassel. *Sizes:* waist: 22 to 30 inches; length: 36 to 43 inches. An extremely beautiful model for wear on dress occasions................**$6.98**

5A48—Same style and color as No. 5A21, but made in Misses' and Small Women's sizes. Waist: 22 to 28 inches. Lengths: 33 to 35 inches.................. **$6.98**

5A22—Carefully Tailored Skirt of Good Quality Serge. A practical model, made with a button-trimmed belt and buttoned patch pockets. The front panel is stitched to below the yoke and there released to acquire necessary fulness. In back the panel is continued the full length of skirt. Convenient side front closing. *Colors:* Black or navy. *Sizes:* waist: 22 to 30 inches. Lengths: 36 to 43 inches.................. **$3.98**

5A22
$3⁹⁸
SERGE

Unparalleled Skirt Values

Samples of Perry-Dame skirt materials will be sent you gladly, FREE.

5A24—Beautiful Dress Skirt of Striped Satin in an excellent weight. Satin is one of the season's favorite skirt fabrics. Cut on plain, graceful lines. The pendant patch pockets are prettily gathered and trimmed with satin-covered buttons. The sectional belt extends from the sides across the gathers in back. *Colors:* Navy or black, both with blue stripes. *Sizes:* Waist: 22 to 30 inches. Lengths: 36 to 43 inches.......................**$5.49**

5A54—Same style and colors as No. 5A24, but made in Misses' and Small Women's. Sizes: Waist: 22 to 28 inches. Lengths: 33 to 35 inches.........**$5.49**

5A25
$6 25
All WOOL POPLIN

5A24
5A54
$5 49
STRIPED SATIN

5A25—Side and Box Plaited Skirt of High Grade All Wool Poplin. The vogue for stitching is seen in the eight rows which encircle the bottom of the skirt above the hem. Stitching also outlines the neat buttoned belt at waist. The front and back sections are box plaited, while the sides are laid in side plaits. *Colors:* Black with black, or navy with gold stitching. *Sizes:* Waist: 22 to 30 inches. Lengths: 36 to 43 in.......**$6.25**

5A26
$5 98
MEN'S WEAR WOOL SERGE

5A26—Sport Skirt of Fine Quality Men's Wear Wool Serge. Gracefully shirred beneath the yoke belt at back to give sufficient breadth. Buttons trim the belt at the side front seams and also at the back. They form the side front closing. The smart slashed pockets are trimmed with a small silk embroidered arrow. *Colors:* Black, navy or gold. *Sizes:* Waist: 22 to 30 inches. Lengths: 36 to 43 inches.........**$5.98**

Newest Style Skirts

5A27
$3 59
SERGE,

5A28
$6 50
MEN'S WEAR
WOOL SERGE

5A29
5A50
$4 69
PLAIDED FINE SERGE

5A30
$6 29
WOOL POPLIN

Smart Wash Skirts for Women and Misses

5A38
5A61
89¢
LINENE

5A38—Skirt of Finest Quality White Linene. Shallow yoke at top appears almost like a belt. Button-trimmed pointed patch pockets. Button closing through overlapping front seam. *Sizes:* 22 to 30 waist. Lengths: 36 to 43 inches. . . . . **.89**

5A61—Same skirt as 5A38, but in small women's and misses' sizes. . . . . **.89**

5A36—Skirt of Superior Quality White Linen Crash. Open all the way down the front and fastened with pearl buttons. Slight gathers beneath stitched belt in back to insure fit across the hips. *Sizes:* 22 to 30 waist. Lengths: 36 to 43 inches. **$1.79**

5A60—Same skirt, but in small women's and misses' sizes. **$1.79**

9A55—Carefully Tailored Khaki Riding Middy Coat. The collar, cuffs, belt and pockets are of the material. The back has a deep box plait through which the belt passes. Closes through front panel with bone buttons. Button-trimmed belt, patch pockets and cuffs. Natural colored khaki only. *Sizes:* 32 to 44 bust measure. **$1.79**

5A66—Divided Riding Skirt of Khaki. Open all the way down the front for convenience in riding astride. Slot seam from belt to yoke depth in back insures neat fit across hips. Stitched belt. *Sizes:* 22 to 30 waist. Lengths: 33 to 43. Natural colored khaki only. **$2.49**

5A36
5A60
$1.79
LINEN
CRASH

RIDING
MIDDY
9A55
$1.79

5A39—Sport Skirt of Awning Striped French Linon. An excellent wearing material. A slip-on model, which buttons all the way down the front. The deep patch pockets finished with button-trimmed points. Beneath the stitched belt at back rows of shirring insure smooth fit across hips. *Colors:* Black, blue, rose or green with white stripes. *Sizes:* 22 to 30 inches waist. Lengths: 36 to 43 inches. **$1.89**

5A58—Same skirt, but in small women's and misses' sizes: 22 to 28 waist. Lengths: 33 to 35. . . . . **$1.89**

5A40—Ideal Summer Skirt of Serviceable Natural Colored Beach Cloth. Readily laundered. A plain tailored model which closes through the overlapping front seam. Slight gathers at back beneath the belt which passes through loops and fastens in front. The patch pockets are cut in unusual outline, being suspended from the waist and trimmed with small pearl buttons. *Sizes:* 22 to 30 inches waist. Lengths: 36 to 43 inches. **$1.59**

5A59—Same style and material, but in small women's and misses' sizes: 22 to 28 inches waist. Lengths: 33 to 35 inches. **$1.59**

5A39
5A58
$1.89
STRIPED
FRENCH
LINON

5A40
5A59
$1.59
BEACH
CLOTH

5A66
$2.49
KHAKI
RIDING
SKIRT

5A31
5A37
$1.25
TUB
GABARDINE

5A32
5A62
$1.00
WASH
SHEPHERD
CHECK

5A31—Serviceable Skirt of Firmly Woven White Tub Gabardine, which may be laundered without the slightest hesitancy. The belt is formed by shirrings and a heading of the material. The closing is accomplished by large bone buttons, through the overlapping front seam. Slashed pockets at each side. Sizes: 22 to 30 inches waist. Lengths: 36 to 43 inches.. **$1.25**

5A37—Same as 5A31, in Misses' and Small Women's Sizes. Waist: 22 to 28. Lengths: 33 to 35.............. **$1.25**

5A32—Neatly Made Skirt of Black and White Wash Shepherd Check. A smart, plain model, ideal for morning wear. Firmly stitched belt of the material. Side front button closing. Convenient patch pockets with button-trimmed pointed tabs of the material. Sizes: 22 to 30 inches. waist. Lengths: 36 to 43 inches.. **$1.00**

5A62—Same Style and Colors as 5A32, but in Misses' and Small Women's Sizes: 22 to 28 inches waist. Lengths: 33 to 35 inches........................, **$1.00**

5A33
5A63
$1.19
WASH
CORDUROY

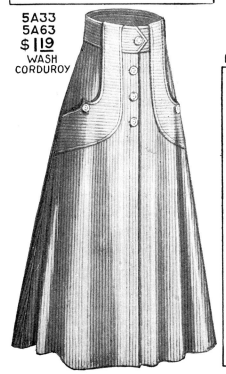

5A34
5A64
$3.19
STRIPED
BEACH CLOTH

5A35
5A65
$1.49
RAMIE
LINENE

5A34—Smart Skirt of Wear-resisting Awning Striped Beach Cloth. Dust shedding. Easily laundered. Gathered patch pockets with button-trimmed band. Opened all the way down and closed with novelty buttons. Gathers at back beneath belt. Colors: Gray and natural or tan and natural stripes. Sizes: 22 to 30 inches waist. Lengths: 36 to 43 inches........ **$3.19**

5A64—Same as 5A34, in Misses' and Small Women's Sizes...... **$3.19**

5A33—Cool and Comfortable Skirt of White Wash Corduroy of Splendid Quality. The pendant patch pockets are most unusual in shape, and are trimmed with pearl buttons. Similar buttons effect the front closing through an overlapping seam. Neatly stitched belt at waist passes through loops. Plain tailored back. Sizes: 22 to 30 inches waist. Lengths: 36 to 43 inches........................... **$1.19**

5A63—Same as 5A33, in Misses' and Small Women's Sizes...... **$1.19**

5A35—Tub Skirt of Extra Quality White Ramie Linene. Trimmed at one side of front closing with button tabs to match patch pocket. Gathers beneath belt at back. Sizes: 22 to 30 waist. Lengths: 36 to 43 inches. **$1.49**

5A65—Same as 5A35, in Misses' and Small Women's Sizes......... **$1.49**

SEE COMPLETE INDEX ON PAGE 125

Stylishly Charming Skirts for Misses and Small Women

5A41—Gracefully Side-Plaited Skirt of Fine Chiffon Panama. One of the season's highly favored materials for fine dress skirts. A plaited frill of the Panama appears above the stitched, button-trimmed belt. Neatly finished and carefully made throughout. *Colors:* Black or navy. *Sizes:* 22 to 28 waist. Lengths: 32 to 37 inches. . **$3.98**

5A44—A Well-tailored Skirt of Serviceable Wool and Cotton Serge with detachable chatelaine patch pockets. One of the season's newest style details. The skirt is made with a neat slot seam in front, and finished at the top with a frill of the material. Beneath the narrow stitched belt, rows of shirring give requisite fulness. *Colors:* Black or navy. *Sizes:* 22 to 28 waist. Lengths: 32 to 37 inches. . . **$2.98**

5A42
$3.29
NOVELTY CHECK

5A43
$4.25
ALL WOOL SERGE

5A41
$3.98
CHIFFON PANAMA

5A44
$2.98
SERGE

5A42—An Ideal Sport Skirt of Gold, Black and White Novelty Check. An extremely smart model. Made with deep pointed, gathered patch pockets, finished with a heading and button-trimmed band of the material. The front is cut to flare properly, while sufficient fulness for the back is acquired through the introduction of shirring beneath the belt. Convenient side closing. *Sizes:* 22 to 28 waist. Lengths: 32 to 37 inches. **$3.29**

5A43—Smartly Designed Skirt of Superior Quality All Wool French Serge. Two box plaits comprise the front panel and the side back gores, between which side plaits are stitched to the hips. Then released they fall in charming side plaits to the hem. The gathered pouch pockets are finished with a button-trimmed band and a heading of the material. *Colors:* Black or navy. *Sizes:* 22 to 28 waist. Lengths: 32 to 37 inches. **$4.25**

Samples of Perry-Dame Skirt materials will be sent you gladly, FREE.

WHY WORRY ABOUT THOSE COOL SPRING DAYS — WHEN YOU CAN HAVE A COAT LIKE THIS!

Never before have we been able to offer you Coats of such striking beauty and remarkable value as we do this season.

Coats in the Newest Materials.
Coats of the Season's Latest Colorings.
The Stylish New Sport Coats.
Handsome Coats for Dress Occasions.

We show you all these and many more. All with the PERRY-DAME GUARANTEE.

Description of the Handsome Coat Shown on This Page

3A8—Latest Model Coat of Very Superior Quality All Wool Poplin. Fashion's demands for gay colors, rich materials, and distinctive details are fully complied with in this carefully designed coat. The comfortable raglan sleeve is finished with a scalloped-edged button-trimmed cuff of the poplin. The slashed pockets are neat and roomy enough for the kerchief and purse. The deep square collar is slashed in points over the shoulders and finished with smooth setting notched revers. It is also trimmed with buttons and outlined with rows of black stitching. The back of the coat achieves grace and beauty of line. Below the sectional belt at the center back it falls in a broad panel. The side back gores are very slightly gathered to give just the proper amount of additional flare. The double belt at either side of the front confines the fulness of the side gores. *Colors:* Apple green, mustard, navy or black. *Sizes:* 32 to 46 bust measure. Length: 42 inches.................................. **$11.98**

How to Order Your Right Size Coat

It is an easy matter for you to get a perfect-fitting Coat at Perry, Dame & Co.'s. Take your Bust Measure over your shirtwaist with an accurate tape measure, making no allowance and we will send you your right size. The length of each coat is stated in each description.

Samples of Perry-Dame Coat Materials will be sent you gladly, FREE.

3A8
$1198

ALL WOOL POPLIN

Three Stylish · Coats of Rich Materials

3A11—Up-to-date Coat of High Grade All Wool Cheviot Serge. Cut on new and extremely becoming lines. Gathers at the waist in back attain a graceful flare for the skirt portion. The belt around the back and sides is outlined by rows of stitching in a contrasting color. In front the narrow stitched folds of the material slides through reinforced buttonholes in the belt and fastens in the latest "throw-tie" manner. Rows of stitching also ornament the deep collar, the cuffs and the pointed patch pockets. The closing is effected by novelty buttons in a shade to match. *Colors:* Apple green, old gold, old rose, or navy. *Sizes:* 32 to 46 inches bust measure. Length: 38 inches...............................**$11.98**

3A9
$8 98
FINE QUALITY SERGE

3A10
$15 98
WOOL VELOUR

3A9—Trim Appearing Coat of Very Superior Quality All Wool Serge. Button-trimmed belt confines the fulness at the back and fastens in front to the smartly modeled pockets. The deep square collar is neatly finished with rows of stitching and trimmed with fine bone buttons. The turned-back cuffs of the material are cut in pointed outline and are also button trimmed. Extra wide facing of the material and all seams carefully bound. *Colors:* Navy, green or black. *Sizes:* 32 to 46 bust measure. Length: 36 inches. The excellence of the material and the style and finish of this coat make it an exceptionally good value—one which Perry, Dame feels especially glad to be able to offer you................................**$8.98**

3A10—Handsome Coat of Finest Quality All Wool Velour. Carefully tailored throughout and lined to the waist with Paisley pattern silk. The wide shapely revers and the deep sailor collar are made of finest White French Serge, which also forms the extra deep front facing, extending to the bottom of the coat. Stitched belt appears at waist, beneath which slight gathers secure desirable fulness for the back. In accord with popular demand rows of stitching trim the lower portion of the coat, the patch pockets, the cuffs and also the ends of the "throw-tie" belt. Large pearl button closing. *Colors:* Navy, apple green, mustard, or wistaria. *Sizes:* 32 to 46 bust measure. Length: 38 inches....**$15.98**

Samples of Perry-Dame Coat materials will be sent you gladly, FREE.

3A11
$11 98
All WOOL
CHEVIOT SERGE

Women's Coats of Exclusive Style

3A12—Up-to-date Sport Coat of Rich Appearing Velvet Corduroy. Superior quality and made throughout with special attention to every detail. The stitched belt at waist adjusts the fulness. It crosses in front and fastens to the patch pockets at either side. The well-shaped collar is made in one with the revers and may be worn buttoned close to the throat, as shown, or turned back in rever fashion. The pointed turned-back cuffs of the material are trimmed with self-covered buttons. *Colors:* Coral, Copenhagen or white. *Sizes:* 32 to 46 bust measure. Length: 34 inches.............. **$7.48**

3A13—General Utility Coat of Well-wearing Velour Plaid, black and white with a gold overplaid—a most harmonious blend of colors. Beneath the belt at waist, the slight gathers procure necessary fulness. The deep square collar has notched revers. The patch pockets are roomy and convenient. Buttons to harmonize form the closing and trim the belt and the turned-back cuffs of the material. *Colors:* As described. *Sizes:* 32 to 46 bust measure. Length: 38 inches..................................**$8.48**

3A14—Serviceable Coat of High Grade All Wool Serge, with extra deep yoke lining of the material. Gathers beneath the belt at the back and sides achieve necessary flare for the lower portion. The belt crosses in front and fastens to large bone buttons. The cuffs and the deep square collar of the material are trimmed with rows of stitching and small bone buttons. *Sizes:* 32 to 46 bust measure. Length: 42 inches. *Colors:* Navy or apple green with gold stitching, or mustard or black with black.............. **$10.98**

3A14
$10.98
All WOOL SERGE

3A15—Handsome Coat of Superior Quality All Silk Jersey. The deep square back collar and the cuffs are of White All Silk Jersey. The same material is again utilized as folds on the patch pockets. The new style "throw-tie" belt is finished with long white silk tassels. Triple rows of shirring in back give requisite fulness. Self-covered buttons form the fastening, which may be continued close to the throat or left open, as illustrated. The beautiful lustre and heavy weight of the material make this an unusual price opportunity. *Colors:* Gold, Copenhagen, rose or green. *Sizes:* 32 to 46 bust measure. Length: 32 inches........... **$10.98**

3A15
$10.98
SILK JERSEY

3A12
$7.48
VELVET CORDUROY

3A13
$8.48
NOVELTY PLAID MIXTURE

Smartly Designed Coats   for Spring and Summer

3A18—Handsome Coat of Durable All Wool Velour in the Newest Spring Shades: Crushed raspberry, apple green, mustard or Copenhagen. The stitching on the collar, cuffs and patch pockets is of silk in a contrasting color. Smoked pearl buttons effect the closing and trim the cuffs. The throw-tie belt passes through loops at the waist and leaves the adjustment of the fulness to the wearer's discretion. *Sizes:* 32 to 46 inches bust measure. Length: 36 inches......... **$11.98**

This is the Season's Ideal Sport Coat.

Samples of Perry-Dame Coat Materials will be sent you gladly, FREE.

EXTRA QUALITY ALL WOOL SERGE
3A16
$10⁴⁸

TAFFETA SILK
3A17
$12⁵⁰

3A16—Fashionable Coat of Extra High Grade All Wool Serge. Carefully tailored throughout and presenting the latest style features. Extra wide facing of the material. The novelly cut belt is made with a crossed double section both front and back. The double serge collar is well shaped and has a detachable overlay of white figured silk. The patch pockets are cut in the new pendant fashion, extending from beneath the belt. Pretty mottled buttons trim the belt and cuffs and form the closing. *Sizes:* 32 to 46 inches bust measure. Length: 42 inches. *Colors:* Black, navy or Copenhagen............. **$10.48**

3A17 — Beautiful Dress Coat of Finest Black Silk Taffeta. Fashioned in the very latest vogue and pleasingly trimmed with a delightful shade of Forest Green Silk Repp. Outlined with rows of black stitching it supplies the overlay above the collar of the material and appears as a fold on the turned-back cuffs. The shirring at the waist in back is trimmed with silk-covered buttons and secures necessary fulness. Throw-tie belt and buttons of silk taffeta. Deep-pointed patch pockets lined to prevent wear and trimmed with buttons. *Sizes:* 32 to 46 inches bust measure. Length: 37 inches........ **$12.50**

WOOL VELOUR
3A18
$11⁹⁸

Women's Coats in the   Season's Newest Colors

3A1—Superior Quality All Wool Poplin Coat. Most carefully tailored. The deep collar has an insert of contrasting colored silk which makes it wonderfully attractive. The well shaped back has a double belt, similar to the one in front. Button trimmed cuffs of the material have a narrow silk insert. The shirred pockets are lined with silk and set in the coat and finished with a plain band of the material at the top. Deep facing of self material. *Colors:* Apple green, Hague blue, mustard, the season's newest colors, and navy or black. *Sizes:* 32 to 46 bust measure. Back length about 38 inches...... **$10.75**

3A2
$15⁹⁸

3A3
$13⁹⁸

3A1
$10⁷⁵

3A2—Sport Coat of Excellent Closely Woven All Wool Jersey. In back the inverted plaits fall loosely and gracefully below the belt. Deep front yoke is very effective. Gathers at sides procure just the right fulness. New "throw-tie" front belt; button trimmed strap at back. Tabs of White All Wool Jersey trim the pockets. The cuffs and collar are also of White All Wool Jersey —the collar has a deep band of the material at its outer edge. Novelty buttons with pearl centers. Deep front facing of self material. *Colors:* Gold, rose, wistaria or Copenhagen. *Sizes:* 32 to 46 bust measure. Back length about 36 inches....... **$15.98**

3A3—Decidedly Distinctive Coat of High Grade Wool Velour. The season's most popular material for Separate Coats, and Suits. Finely tailored on grace giving lines secured through the introduction of triple rows of shirring on each side. Coat may be worn open, as illustrated, or buttoned close to the throat. Fine pearl buttons fasten the double strap belt at front and back of coat. Deep front facing of self material. The collar and cuffs of the material are edged with a deep band of White Wool Velour. *Colors:* Coral, mustard, apple green or Copenhagen. *Sizes:* 32 to 46 bust measure. Back length about 38 inches. **$13.98**

Four Moderately Priced Exceptional Coats

3A7—Fine Quality All Wool Serge Coat. The novel belt crosses in front and fastens to the pockets. Wide facing of self material. Serge collar with contrasting colored silk repp overlay, outlined with rows of stitching. *Colors:* Navy, Copenhagen, mustard or black. *Sizes:* 32 to 46 bust. Back length about 42 inches.... **$8.98**

3A5 **$9.98**

3A5—High grade Cheviot Sport Coat. Small buttons and rows of contrasting stitching trim the collar, cuffs, belt and pockets. *Colors:* Crushed raspberry, apple green, old gold, or navy. *Sizes:* 32 to 46 bust measure. Length 36 in. **$9.98**

3A6 **$10.98**

3A4 **$11.98**

3A7 **$8.98**

3A4—All Wool Poplin Coat. Slightly gathered side gores below waist. Collar of two toned silk. Sectional belt, patch pockets. *Colors:* Apple green, mustard, Copenhagen, navy or black. *Sizes:* 32 to 46 bust. Length 40 inches.......... **$11.98**

3A6—Coat of Velour Check. Raglan sleeves. Velvet and Broadcloth collar. Velvet tabs on pockets. Double belt. *Colors:* Green and purple or green and gold. *Sizes:* 32 to 46 bust. Length 32 inches....... **$10.98**

New Coats of Unusual Design

Samples of these Perry-Dame Coat materials will be sent you gladly, FREE.

3A19
$15⁹⁸
ALL WOOL
POPLIN
PAISLEY
LINED

3A20
$14⁹⁸
WOOL
VELOUR

3A19—A very Superior Coat of All Wool Poplin in the latest vogue. Lined to the waist with Paisley Seco Silk. The smooth setting round collar has an overlay of scalloped edged white broadcloth. At the back, a deep box plait is bordered by graceful side plaits stitched from below the waist to hip depth, thereby contributing modish fulness to the skirt of the coat. Satin lined pendant patch pocket hung from beneath the underarm seam. Double cuffs of the material with gilt ornamented button trimming. The same buttons trim the belt and form the closing, which may be effected as illustrated, or buttoned close to the throat. New "throw-tie" belt. *Sizes:* 32 to 46 bust measure. Length: 42 inches. *Colors:* Navy, apple green, mustard or black. A stylish coat of unusual beauty and quality.............................**$15.98**

3A20—Finely Tailored Coat of All Wool Velour. The season's most popular material, soft and velvety and a most excellent Spring weight. The graceful back is stitched from shoulder to waist depth. Below this point it falls in inverted plaits at either side of the box plait which extends from the neck to the hem, so accomplishing long lines and pleasing fulness. The new double belt has rows of stitching in conformity with that which ornaments the patch pockets and the cuffs. The deep collar has smartly rounded corners. *Sizes:* 32 to 46 bust measure. Length: 36 inches. *Colors:* Navy, apple green, Copenhagen or mustard.........**$14.98**

Coats of Exceptional Value and Style

3A21—Smart Coat of Fine Quality Shepherd Check practically all wool. Extra wide self facing. The collar and cuffs have an inlay of heavy Green Silk Repp. The new style double belt at waist confines the fulness. The patch pockets and cuffs are trimmed with green and black novelty buttons, similar to those which effect the closing. *Colors:* Black and White Check trimmed with green. *Sizes:* 32 to 46 bust measure. Length: 40 inches. Check Coats are always in high favor. This season they are more popular than ever............ **$7.98**

3A22
$9⁹⁸
All WOOL POPLIN

3A22—Dressy Sport Coat of Superior All Wool Poplin. Cut with generous flare, in the latest vogue. The deep square collar, the cuffs, belt and patch pockets have rows of silk stitching in contrasting color. The patch pockets are new style, being suspended from the belt at waist. The coat may be worn open as pictured, or buttoned close. *Colors:* Navy, green, mustard or black with color stitching. *Sizes:* 32 to 46 bust measure. Length: 34 inches.. **$9.98**

3A21
$7⁹⁸
WOOL CHECK

3A23
$14⁹⁸
WOOL VELOUR

3A23—A very Superior Coat of Excellent Quality All Wool Velour. Up to date in every detail. A stitched band of white broad cloth and buttons adorn the cuffs, patch pockets and square collar. The back is made with a shoulder yoke, beneath which the material falls in a broad box plait. It is confined at the waist by the button trimmed belt which extends from the side back seams and fastens "throw-tie" in front. *Colors:* Crushed raspberry, mustard, apple green or navy. *Sizes:* 32 to 46 bust measure. Length: 42 inches. **$14.98**

Women's Coats for All Occasions

3A24—Modish Coat of Softly Woven Scotch Tweed of excellent quality and weight, practically all wool. Deep front facing. The gracefully rounded collar is of Velour Broadcloth combined with the material and trimmed with buttons of a like combination. Smart, loose fitting back. The Cross Strap Belt confines the fulness in front and buttons to the patch pockets. Turned-back cuffs of the material trimmed with a button complete the sleeves. *Colors:* Gray or brown mixture. *Sizes:* 32 to 46 bust measure. Length: 42 inches......... **$9.50**

3A25
$6.98
FLANNEL COATING

3A24
$9.50
TWEED

3A25—Fashionable Coat of Light Weight, Flannel Coating. The collar, cuffs and patch pockets are of contrasting colored materials. The belt at waist adjusts the fulness. Novelty buttons trim the cuffs and form the front closing. *Colors:* Green, Copenhagen, gold or rose. *Sizes:* 32 to 46 bust. Length: 34 inches................. **$6.98**

3A26—Carefully Tailored Coat of Superior Quality All Wool Jersey. The side belts and the deep pendant patch pockets are cut in novel outline and trimmed with pearl buttons. The comfortable raglan sleeves are finished with deep, button-trimmed cuffs of the material. The smooth setting square back collar has notched revers and may be worn buttoned close to the throat, or open, as shown in the small view. *Colors:* Copenhagen, apple green or old gold. *Sizes:* 32 to 46 bust measure. Length: 36 inches. An excellent Perry-Dame Value.. **$12.65**

3A26
$12.65
All WOOL JERSEY

Women's Spring and Summer Coats

3A28—Faultlessly Made Coat of High Grade All Wool Velour. Deep front facing of the material. Slight gathers are introduced beneath the belt at the back. The patch pockets offer security in their button fastening. The gracefully rounded collar and the cuffs are outlined by rows of stitching. *Colors:* Copenhagen, gold, green or navy. *Sizes:* 32 to 46 inches bust measure. Length: 42 inches. High grade material cut on generous lines and neatly finished throughout........ **$11.98**

3A27
$12⁹⁸
ALL WOOL POPLIN

3A27—An Exceptionally Moderate Priced Coat of Service-giving All Wool Poplin. The deep collar has Silk Repp overlay. The belt fastens at one side, and is trimmed across the back with buttons. Beneath the belt slight gathers give requisite flare. Neatly finished slashed pockets. Turned-back cuffs trimmed with buttons. *Colors:* Apple green, mustard, black or navy, with silk collar in contrasting color. *Sizes:* 32 to 46 bust measure. Length: 42 inches................ **$12.98**

3A28
$11⁹⁸
WOOL VELOUR

3A29
$7⁴⁸
All WOOL SERGE

3A30
$6⁴⁸
CHINCHILLA

3A29—Trim-looking Coat of Finely-woven All Wool Serge. The novelly cut collar has an overlay of contrasting colored silk and is trimmed with novelty buttons. The turned-back cuffs of the material and the back section of the belt are bound with Soutache braid. The deep patch pockets have button-trimmed, deep-pointed tabs of the material. *Sizes:* 32 to 46 inches bust measure. Length: 38 inches. *Colors:* Navy, black, Copenhagen or mustard.... **$7.48**

3A30—Jaunty Sport Coat of Chinchilla, carefully tailored and made extra full. Finished with a wide facing of self material. A delightful new note is the piping of White Silk Soutache Braid which binds the edges of the collar, cuffs, belt and front. The slashed pockets are finished top and bottom with white silk stays. The belt passes through loops at the waist as it distributes the fulness. White only. *Sizes:* 32 to 46 inches bust measure. Length: 34 inches.... **$6.48**

Stylish Coats for Misses and Small Women

3A202—Modish Coat of Closely Woven Black and White Shepherd Check. It is cut on loose fitting lines, the fulness being adjusted by the sectional belt at back and front. The deep square back collar is pleasingly finished with a wide band of Emerald Green Silk Repp, trimmed with novelty buttons. Similar buttons trim the belt and effect the closing. *Sizes:* 14 to 20 years. Length: 38 inches. An exceptional coat for all season wear.........**$4.98**

3A203—Well-made Sport Coat of Flannel Coating, white ground with combination over plaid. The belt may be worn buttoned across the front, or back, as desired. The square collar may be worn open, as pictured, displaying the notched revers, or buttoned close to the throat. *Sizes:* 14 to 20 years. Length: 32 inches. An excellent coat for wear at outdoor games on cool Spring and Summer days... **$4.48**

3A203
$4 48
FLANNEL COATING

Send for **FREE** Samples of these Coat Materials.

3A202
$4 98
SHEPHERD CHECK

SIZES:
14 yaers, 32 bust;
16 years, 34 bust;
18 years, 36 bust;
20 years, 38 bust;
See Page 146

3A201—Handsome Coat of All Wool Velour, specially designed, of rich material in the latest colors: Crushed Raspberry, Mustard, Apple Green, or Navy—for those who lean toward the conservative shades in dress. The deep collar, cuffs, sectional belt and extremely new model pendant pockets all show rows of black stitching. Self-covered buttons with black satin rims. *Sizes:* 14 to 20 years. Length: 34 inches.......... **$10.98**

3A204—Coat of All Wool Poplin. The patch pockets have a long tab buttoned fastening. The collar has an overlay of velour cheviot stitched in contrasting color. Sectional belt back and front. Button-trimmed tabs on back seams. *Colors:* Navy with Copenhagen collar, Copenhagen or mustard with white; or apple green or black with mustard collar. Length: 36 inches. *Sizes:* 14 to 20 years. **$9.98**

3A201
$10 98
WOOL VELOUR

3A204
$9 98
ALL WOOL POPLIN

3A206—Serviceable Coat of Excellent All Wool Serge. Newly designed belt determines the front fulness. Loose fitting back. Convenient patch pockets. Turned-back cuffs of the material have rows of stitching and button trimming. The shallow mannish collar with its notched revers has a white serge overlay with rows of stitching. *Sizes:* 14 to 20 years. Length: 36 inches. *Colors:* Black, navy, Copenhagen or mustard.... **$6.98**

Coats for Misses and Small Women

3A207—Utility Coat of Closely Woven Cotton Worsted Novelty Plaid. A black and white check ground with large Emerald Green Overplaid. The deep collar is bordered at the sides with Emerald Green broadcloth, and trimmed with buttons. The stitched belt at waist is also button trimmed. Deep patch pockets at either side. *Sizes:* 14 to 20 years. Length: 34 inches......... **$4.98**

SIZES:
14 years, 32 bust;
16 years, 34 bust;
18 years, 36 bust;
20 years, 38 bust.

3A206
$6.98
ALL WOOL SERGE

3A207
$4.98
NOVELTY PLAID

3A205
$6.98
ALL WOOL MIXTURE

3A205—Well Made Coat of Gray and Brown All Wool Mixture. Pleasing color contrast is found in the band of Emerald Green broadcloth which trims the deep collar and the turned-back cuffs. It also supplies the deep tab which forms a button fastening for the roomy patch pockets. The fulness is adjusted by means of the stitched belt. *Sizes:* 14 to 20 years. Length: 38 inches.................. **$6.98**

3A208—Smart Sport Coat of High Grade Velour Cheviot. A new and fashionable model. The double front belt of Forest Green Velvet extends from the belt of the material at the back. Green velvet border on the deep square collar. The deep patch pockets show tabs of the material with smoked pearl button trimming, similar to the button trimming on the collar, cuffs and belt. *Colors:* Red, navy or Copenhagen. *Sizes:* 14 to 20 years. Length: 34 inches.. **$7.98**

3A208
$7.98
VELOUR CHEVIOT

Three Smart Raincoats and a Linen Duster

2A3—Raincoat of Well-rubberized Jacquard Silk. Ventilating eyelets beneath the arms. The deep belt at waist controls the fulness. Neatly inserted slashed pockets. Coat may be worn buttoned to the throat, or left open to form revers. The seams throughout are all securely stitched and cemented. *Sizes:* 32 to 46 bust measure. Length 54 inches. *Color:* Jasper gray.... **$5.75**

2A1—Well-made Raincoat of Rubberized Tan Cotton Cashmere. The back is loose fitting. The fulness of the front is adjusted by the aid of the stitched belt at waist. Smart patch pockets with securely buttoned flaps. Strap at wrist assures a snug-fitting cuff. A firmly stitched, neatly finished coat which insures dry warmth and comfort. *Sizes:* 32 to 46 bust measure. Length 52 inches.................... **$2.98**

2A2
$4.98
POPLIN

2A3
$5.75
JACQUARD
SILK

2A1
$2.98
COTTON
CASHMERE

2A4
$2.98
PURE LINEN
DUSTER

2A4—Carefully tailored Pure Linen Duster. An ideal protection from dust while motoring. The large patch pockets of the linen are completed with pointed turned-back folds. Graceful round collar with notched revers. The well-shaped sleeves have turned-back cuffs of the material. The fulness is distributed to the wearer's liking by means of the stitched belt encircling the waist. Large bone buttons form the closing. *Sizes:* 32 to 46 bust measure. Length 52 inches. *Color:* Natural Linen only. An exceptionally low-priced coat of superior quality and make................. **$2.98**

2A2—A Perry Dame Special is this Finely Made Raincoat of High Grade Poplin. Thoroughly rubberized to afford complete protection from dampness. Every seam securely stitched and cemented. Ventilating eyelets beneath the arms. Deep pockets and utility slits for raising the skirt. Loose-fitting back. The cross strap belt, a new style detail, adjusts the front folds. The closing may be continued close to throat or left open as shown in small view. Turned-back button-trimmed cuffs. *Colors:* Tan or navy. *Sizes:* 32 to 46 bust measure. Length 52 inches..... **$4.98**

OUR GUARANTEE IS ABSOLUTE—SATISFACTION ASSURED

16A8
$3⁹⁸
LIGHTLY
BRUSHED
ANGORA

16A9
$4⁹⁸

16A5
$2⁷⁹

16A6
$2⁷⁵
WOOL
JERSEY
MIDDY

FIBRE
SILK
16A4
$7⁹⁸

16A7
$4⁶⁹
FANCY MERCERIZED
FIBRE TRIMMED

Women's and Misses' Sweaters

16A8—Well Made Sweater of Lightly Brushed Angora. The deep, square back collar is interwoven with bands of white Angora, which lends effective contrast. White Angora also supplies the belt. *Colors:* Copenhagen, rose or apple green. *Sizes:* 32 to 44 inches bust measure........ **$3.98**

16A9—New Model "Shetland Weave" All Wool Sweater. The collar, cuffs, patch pocket trimming and the new "throw-tie" belt are of striped material, which proves an effective contrast. *Colors:* Rose or Copenhagen, striped material to match. *Sizes:* 32 to 44 bust measure. **$4.98**

16A5—Mannish Sweater of Good Weight Merino with a deep roll collar. Just the right weight for wear after outdoor exercise, to guard against the danger of chill. *Colors:* Cardinal red or navy blue. *Sizes:* 32 to 44 inches bust measure........ **$2.79**

16A4—Beautiful Sweater of Flawless Fibre Silk, with a lustrous sheen. The back is made with a deep box plait which is released at waist depth to secure desired fulness. The "throw-tie" belt is drawn through loops of the material and completed with ball ends. The patch pockets are made with box plaits and a fold of white Fibre Silk, to match the material used for the collar and belt. *Colors:* Rose, Copenhagen or gold, combined with white. *Sizes:* 32 to 44 bust measure. An exceedingly handsome sweater for Spring and Summer wear.................... **$7.98**

16A6—Trim Fitting Sport Middy of All Wool Jersey. The collar, cuffs and hem are of White Worsted, a pleasing contrast. White cord lacing at the neck and sides. *Colors:* Copenhagen, rose or apple green. *Sizes:* 6 to 14 years. Light in weight, yet warm and comfortable................ **$2.75**

16A7—Fancy Mercerized Sport Coat of Fibre Silk and Mercerized Cotton in an extremely pretty new weave. The body of the garment is a checked material in either rose or Copenhagen color combinations. The belt at back, the trimming on the patch pockets and on the cuffs is of the Fibre Silk in a harmonizing shade. Novelty buttons trim the belt and patch pockets, and form the front closing. *Sizes:* 32 to 44 inches bust measure........ **$4.69**

Women's and Misses' Sweaters

16A11
$3⁵⁹

16A10
$4¹⁹

16A14
$3⁶⁹

16A11—Firmly Woven All Wool Sweater. Made with button trimmed "throw-tie" belt, with tassel ends. This belt buttons at the sides and may be detached. Convenient pockets. *Colors:* Navy blue, cardinal red or apple green. *Sizes:* 32 to 44 bust measure.............. **$3.59**

16A10—Smart Appearing Jersey Sport Coat. The smooth fitting collar is made with two deep points at the back and outlined with a band of the material interwoven with black stripes, which lend pleasing contrast. The slashed pockets are also treated in a similar manner. Slight gathers at the waist in back. *Colors:* Copenhagen blue, rose, or apple green with black trimming. *Sizes:* 32 to 44 bust measure...... **$4.19**

16A14—Firmly Woven Worsted and Cotton Sweater. White stripes on Copenhagen, rose, or apple green ground. White Worsted furnishes the belt and cuffs and the band which extends around the neck and down the front of the garment. *Sizes:* 32 to 44 inches bust measure.......... **$3.69**

16A13—Excellent Sweater of "Zephyr" Wool. The collar is of White Zephyr, which also borders the front of the coat. It is seen again on the patch pockets, and is employed in the making of the "throw-tie" belt, with its tassel ends. *Colors:* Copenhagen, rose, or apple green, with white. *Sizes:* 32 to 44 inches bust measure................ **$3.98**

16A15—Delightfully Soft and Lustrous Fibre Silk, plated on a durable cotton back, supplies this Handsome Sweater. The slightly gathered back gives desirable fulness. The collar, cuffs and belt are of Gold Colored Fibre Silk. The same material is again used for the buttons and for the pointed tabs on the roomy patch pockets. *Colors:* Copenhagen and gold or rose and gold. *Sizes:* 32 to 44 bust measure... **$5.29**

16A12—Good Weight Worsted Sweater for girls from 6 to 14 years. Made with roll collar and turned-back cuffs. Buttoned belt at waist. The patch pockets show folds of the Worsted. *Colors:* Copenhagen, rose or white....... **$2.39**

Softly Woven Sweaters
Designed With a View to
Style and Comfort

$3⁹⁸
16A13

16A15
$5²⁹

16A12
$2³⁹

Women's Latest Style Hats
of Superior Quality

Perry, Dame & Company specialize in Women's Millinery. Every model is designed with the object of offering you the latest styles at the lowest possible prices.

7A2
$2<u>98</u>

7A1
$3<u>49</u>

7A3
$4<u>98</u>

A Smart Tailored Hat of Fancy Woven Straw Braid

7A2—Smart Close Fitting Hat cleverly fashioned from fine quality Silk Braid in a new weave. The braid is prettily plaited about the side crown while the top of crown is smooth—making a very pleasing contrast. A cluster of two-toned June roses combined with foliage and a fine Horsehair Aigrette supply the neat trimming at the front. *Colors:* Black, navy, white, myrtle green or old rose, each trimmed as described.... **$2.98**

Beautiful Dress Hat with Ostrich Plumes

7A3—Lustrous Silk Braid securely sewn on a well made buckram frame supplies the upper and under brim of this Fashionable Hat. The outer edge of the brim is completed by a flange of good grade Messaline ribbon, softly gathered. Folds of the Messaline ribbon encircle the crown which is also of the silk braid and terminate at one side in a rosette. Here the Ostrich plumes with their long, broad flues and heads are attached to the hat and fall gracefully over the crown and brim. One plume is 16 inches long and the other is 14 inches long. *Colors:* Black, white, Copenhagen and old rose with plumes to match. A very superior hat made with care from excellent materials................... **$4.98**

A Becoming Hat of Horsehair Braid and Chiffon

7A1—A most becoming hat of finely woven Horsehair Braid securely sewn on a Chiffon covered wire frame. Two beautiful large silk, velvet and muslin roses trim the front. Black velvet ribbon is softly twisted about the crown. *Colors:* Black with American Beauty red roses; Copenhagen, white, or old rose with pink roses. A very pretty summery model which will harmonize with most any costume..... **$3.49**

Women's Hats of Distinction

7A5
$2 69

7A6
$3 49

7A7
$2 98

7A9
$2 25

7A4
$2 98

7A10
$2 49

7A8
$3 49

7A6—Youthful Hat of Fancy Woven Silk Braid and Fine Shadow Lace on an indestructible Steel Wire Frame which keeps the hat in shape. Black ribbon Velvet around crown forms a flat bow in back. Linen rose and foliage at side front. *Colors:* All black with red rose; or Copenhagen, old rose or white with white lace and pink rose and foliage.... **$3.49**

7A5—Trim Appearing Hat of Finely Woven Smooth Silk Braid. Gathered satin crown and curled quill of Satin and straw with button trimming. *Colors:* Black, white, navy, Copenhagen or brown............ **$2.69**

7A9—Smart Hat of Soft-finished Horsehair Braid with Satin Tam O'Shanter Crown, trimmed with straw pompom and two quill whips. *Color Combinations:* Black with old rose crown, white with Copenhagen, navy blue with emerald green; or, all black or all white............ **$2.25**

7A8—Superior Quality Leghorn Hat. Top of brim has an insert of Silk and Cotton Crêpe de Chine. Messaline ribbon bands across the crown terminate on the brim in slashed ends. Wreath of American Beauty silk and linen roses and buds combined with foliage. *Colors:* Natural Leghorn Hat with old rose, Copenhagen or black trimming........................ **$3.49**

7A4—Jaunty Hat of smoothly woven Silk Braid. The crown is entirely covered with Satin Duchess. Grosgrain Silk Ribbon sash with fringed ends overhangs the brim. Silk straw buckle. *Colors:* Black with Copenhagen buckle; Copenhagen with navy buckle, or white or old rose with black buckle; also all black.................. **$2.98**

7A7—New Style Coronet Hat of lustrous silk braid finished with a feather-edged braid. High lace Coronet held in shape by wires. Folds of Messaline combined with Velvet leaves and silk berries supply the trimming. *Colors:* black, white, Copenhagen or old rose, all with black lace coronet.................. **$2.98**

7A10—Neat Looking Tricorne Hat of Fine Quality Imported Hemp. Trimmed with a Grosgrain Silk Band and rosette, as shown. *Colors:* White, black, navy, Copenhagen or old rose................ **$2.49**

7A13
$2.69

7A14
$3.79

7A15
$3.49

7A16
$1.98

7A11
$1.98

7A12
$2.49

7A17
$4.98

Hats of Quality

7A15—Chic Hat with new high square crown and small mushroom brim with flat-curled drooping edge. Beautiful Ostrich Shower Pompom and Aigrette. Silk Poplin Ribbon is draped about the crown and made into a small rosette. *Colors:* All black, or Copenhagen and black, black and white, or old rose and white..................... **$3.49**

7A13—Pretty Hat of All Over Shadow Lace on a wire frame. Soft Messaline ribbon is laid in folds around the crown and supplies the large bow, where two red and pink shaded roses are caught in the knot. *Colors:* White lace hat with Copenhagen, old rose or white trimming; or, black lace hat with Alice blue or old rose trimming... **$2.69**

7A14—Close Fitting Flower Hat. The substantial linen roses are gracefully placed over a foundation of silk straw braid and fine foliage. Plaited all silk Faille Ribbon gives high side effect. *Colors:* Black, navy, myrtle green, or white, all with pink roses. **$3.79**

7A17—Gainsborough Hat of Fine Imported Milan Hemp, with graceful brim upturned at one side. Soft Messaline ribbon is draped about the square crown. A beautiful 17 inch plume with long, wide flues is caught at one side with a beautiful pink rose. *Colors:* All black, or black, old rose, or Copenhagen hat with white feather; or white hat with Alice blue ribbon and white feather.................... **$4.98**

New Style Hats

7A11—Sport Hat of Finely Woven Imported Wen Chow Straw of a Natural Linen color. The edge of brim is bound with silk ribbon to match the band around the crown. *Color:* Natural Linen with band and binding in any one of the following: Emerald green, red, national blue or black. All with gold color stripes running through........ **$1.98**

7A16—Durable Hat of Finely Woven Panama with Roman striped novelty draped band tied in a soft knot at the left side. This Panama hat is an exceptional value. It is a hat that may be worn as much for sport as for general wear..... **$1.98**

7A12—Well Made Hat of lustrous Silk Mixture Braid in a beautiful pattern. Folds of satin are placed around the crown. Satin wings with a cluster of small red roses trim the left side and a small bunch of roses are caught on the brim at the left. *Colors:* Black, navy or brown... **$2.49**

7A24 $2**75**

7A20 $1**79**

7A19 $2**59**

7A23 $2**79**

7A18 $2**69**

7A22 $2**98**

7A21 $3**98**

Smart Hats

7A18—High Crown Sailor Hat of Lustrous Straw Braid. The soft folds about the crown and facing are of Silk and Cotton Crêpe de Chine. Beautiful Ostrich Fancy with fine Aigrette and rosette at the side. A cluster of silk and linen June roses trims the other side. *Colors:* All black; white with pink Crêpe de Chine and white feathers and aigrette; black, old rose, or Copenhagen with all white trimmings............ **$2.69**

7A24—High Grade Panama Hat with jauntily rolled brim and slightly pinched crown. Messaline ribbon supplies folds around crown and the bow at side. Wreath of June roses in pastel shades, combined with berries and fine foliage. Inside band. Ribbon trimming in pink, light blue, black or white................. **$2.75**

7A19—Tailored Hat of Silk Straw Braid and Satin Duchess. Military Pompom, caught with a silk ornament. Narrow Satin Duchess brim to match top of crown. *Colors:* Black and white, navy and myrtle, brown and burnt, or all black or all Copenhagen............... **$2.59**

7A21—Dress Hat of Finely Woven Straw Braid, with a handsome Ostrich Feather Band and Messaline ribbon around crown, ending in a large soft bow. Clusters of the new style tinselled berries and leaves nestle in the feather trimming. *Colors:* All black or all white; or navy, old rose or Copenhagen, with white feather band.................... **$3.98**

Newest Models

7A22—Good Quality Satin Duchess Hat with Mushroom Brim. Corded Paisley Satin is applied in a design about the crown and brim in an entirely new and novel effect. *Colors:* Black, navy, white or myrtle green, trimmed with Paisley, or all black............. **$2.98**

7A20—Trim Appearing Hat of Lustrous Silk Finished Braid and Satin Duchess. Smart double bow of Satin and Straw at the side back. The crown is entirely covered by the gathered Satin Duchess. *Colors:* All black, navy and white, black and white, or black and Copenhagen....... **$1.79**

7A23—New Model High Crown Hat of Superior Quality Satin Duchess and Silk Straw Braid. The satin is shirred on the top and side crown. The Braid outlines the top of crown and the brim. The latest vogue in trimming is seen in the satin apples. Satin underbrim. *Colors:* Black, white, navy, brown, or myrtle green, or white satin hat with black braid............ **$2.79**

7A28
$1.69

7A25
$3.69

7A27
$2.75

7A29
$2.49

7A30
$2.29

7A26
$1.79

7A31
$1.49

7A25—Dress Sailor of Smooth Silk Braid and Fine Chiffon. Chiffon transparent flange edged with grosgrain. Indestructible steel wire frame. Satin Duchess facing. Wreath of silk wild roses, buds and foliage. Slashed silk ribbon ends at either side. *Colors:* Black with red roses, or white, Copenhagen or old rose with pink roses or black with white flange and red roses.... **$3.69**

7A29—Stylish Hat of Lustrous Silk Braid and Satin, trimmed with a fine silk and muslin rose with foliage. The crown top is of Satin. The side crown and brim are of Braid. Silk ribbon band with slashed ends. *Colors:* White with Copenhagen, white with old rose, navy with myrtle green, black with white, or all black, all with American Beauty Red rose.............. **$2.49**

7A26—Child's Hat of Silk Braid. Top and gathered facing of art satin. Crown finished with Silk Messaline ribbon, a rosette, and a wreath of Bachelor Buttons in varied colors. Rosettes at sides end in a chin ribbon. *Colors:* Pink, light blue, white, Copenhagen or old rose. **$1.79**

7A27—Good Looking Hat of High Grade Messaline and Silk Straw Braid. The upper brim of Messaline suggests the Tricorne shape. Wings of the messaline finished with a soft knot at one side. The other side shows a cluster of metallic cherries and shaded roses. *Colors:* Black, white, navy or old rose.................. **$2.75**

7A28—Large Sailor Hat of Serviceable Textile Panama combined with figured Art Satin. Pink, light blue or tea-rose yellow flowers on a white ground. Crown and flange of Art Satin. A handsome silk grosgrain band with a large bow with slashed ends fastens at one side with a beautiful hemp ornament....... **$1.69**

7A30—Bleached Java Hat with gracefully drooping brim, trimmed with a velvet ribbon rosette across crown, and clusters of cherries. *Colors:* Emerald green, black, national blue or red velvet trimming. A serviceable hat of exceptional value. A hat that may be worn on any occasion and one that will give the greatest satisfaction... **$2.29**

7A31—Child's Hat of light blue, pink or white Art Satin completely covered with white all over lace, which falls in plaits over the brim. Silk straw braid is twisted about the crown and caught here and there with satin berries covered with gold threads. Silk messaline ribbon double rosette and slashed ends at the back.................. **$1.49**

Women's and Misses' Hats

7A34—Modish Hat of Tuscan Pattern Straw Braid in natural Tuscan color. The satin crown top and edge on brim may be had in black, brown, Copenhagen, myrtle green or old rose with silk braid hand-made flower ornaments to harmonize............... **$1.79**

7A37 $2.49

7A35 $2.98

7A34 $1.79

7A36 $1.95

7A32 $2.98

7A38 $1.69

7A33 $2.49

7A36—Trimly Tailored Hat of Duchess Satin with rolled brim. Raised design in worsted embroidery and tinsel cord ornaments the crown. *Colors:* Black, white, army blue, navy blue, old rose, or gold, with embroidery in harmonizing colors........................ **$1.95**

7A35—Superior Quality, Finely Woven Panama Hat with fitted lining. Trimmed with Satin back Black Velvet Ribbon around the crown and with large pink silk and velvet rose, combined with foliage. This hat is a wonderful bargain. A hat that every woman will look her best in. One that will always give her a stylish appearance..................... **$2.98**

7A38—Imported Manoki Woven Straw Hat. Telescope crown. Mushroom brim with a narrow flange of imported hemp. Band and slashed bow of silk grosgrain ribbon. Inside band. *Colors:* Natural straw with red, national blue, emerald green or white ribbon and hemp flange to match.......... **$1.69**

7A32—Beautiful Dress Hat. Softly gathered Messaline Ribbon supplies the crown and flange. Transparent brim of chiffon, over an indestructible steel wire frame. Linen roses and buds to match combined with velvet ribbon trim the hat. *Colors:* Light blue with blue flowers, black, pink or white, with pink flowers to harmonize.......................... **$2.98**

7A37—Dress Hat of Lustrous Black Silk Straw Braid applied in classical scroll effect around the brim. Folds of black silk about the crown end at the side in a chic rosette. Three excellent quality ostrich tips adorn the left side. A very stylish, neat model. A hat for the conservative woman. *Colors:* All black or black with white tips........................ **$2.49**

7A33—Soft Finished Imported Hemp Sport Hat with jauntily rolled brim. Grosgrain ribbon band and bow, in a color to match the Imported Hemp facing. *Colors:* Red, emerald green, navy blue, Copenhagen or old rose facing, ribbon and Satin inside band, all with white crown and upper brim..................... **$2.49**

7A41
$2⁷⁵

7A43
$3⁹⁸

7A44
$2⁴⁹

7A40
$2⁸⁹

7A39
$2⁹⁸

7A45
$2²⁵

7A42
$1⁹⁸

Superior Quality

7A41—Close Fitting Hat of Beautifully Embossed Silk Braid. The semi-coronet is of fine taffeta plaited over a firm buckram foundation, and is finished w i t h a b u t t o n t r i m m i n g. *Colors:* Black, navy, myrtle green or brown. One of the season's very newest models. A hat that will become most every woman...... **$2.75**

7A44—Natural Colored Leghorn Hat of First Quality, trimmed with Silk Poplin and an Imported Hemp Handmade Black-eyed Susan. The Silk Poplin Band may be had in emerald green, national blue, cardinal red or black............... **$2.49**

7A39—New Style Hat of Silk and Cotton Crêpe de Chine, cleverly combined with Crimped Silk Braid. The Crêpe de Chine appears as an insertion on the brim between rows of the Braid and as a facing. Five clusters of pretty June roses and foliage and moss stems supply the wreath. *Colors:* Black, white, Copenhagen, old rose, or light gray, all with pink roses..... **$2.98**

7A42—Up-to-date Draped Hat of Fine Satin Duchess in plain color, with a piping of Paisley colored satin about the crown and around the lower edge of brim. Two wired points lend desirable height. *Colors:* Black, white, navy, myrtle green or red, all piped with Paisley colors. A typical New York Style with the newest Paisley trimming.......................... **$1.98**

Fashionable Hats

7A45—Effective Dress Hat of Fine Straw Braid and Chiffon. Straw braid crown and chiffon brim, gracefully gathered over a substantial wire frame. The wreath of silk and linen rosebuds is finished at one side with a large rose. *Colors:* Black, with red rose; or white, champagne, pink or light blue with pink rose................ **$2.25**

7A43—Becoming Hat of Smooth Finished Silk Straw Braid with a one-inch Silk Poplin Flange. At the front of the crown, which is completely covered with lilacs and fine foliage, a large silk rose is placed to advantage. *Colors:* White, Copenhagen, old rose or black, all with white lilacs and a pink rose.. **$3.98**

7A40—Imported Hemp Hat of Excellent Quality. Trimmed with a band and "Sun Ray" Rosette of heavy silk ribbon finished with slashed ends and caught with clusters of silk berries, covered with gold threads. *Colors:* Black, old rose, or Copenhagen; or, black a n d w h i t e, o r s a n d a n d brown...................... **$2.89**

7A47—Beautifully made Hat of Finely Woven Tagal Hemp deftly combined with Fine Satin. The imported hemp forms the upper and lower brim and also the top of crown. The Satin comprises the 2-inch flange and the side of crown. A tasteful combination of two-colored satin ribbon with Paisley Art Colored Flowers appear at the front of Hat. *Colors:* All black or all white; or light blue, light gray, pink or bottle green combinations. **$4.98**

7A49—Gracefully Shaped Tricorne Hat of Fine Silk Braid with an overlay of Paisley Pattern Voile on the crown and brim. A circle of silk braid trims the top of crown from which the voile falls in soft folds to the brim where it is confined by a band which extends around the crown and terminates at one side in a braid and voile ornament. *Colors:* Navy, black, white, myrtle green, or old rose, with the Paisley voile........................ **$2.79**

7A49
$2.79

7A47
$4.98

7A51
$5.49

7A46
$6.49

7A52
$3.29

7A48
$2.25

7A50
$2.49

7A52—Lustrous Silk Braid Hat. The crown is of bands of soft Messaline Satin Ribbon terminating in slashed ends, caught with a braid ornament at one side. A wreath of silk and linen roses entwined with pretty foliage encircles the brim. *Colors:* White, with Copenhagen or with old rose, black with Alice blue, navy with green, or all black, all with American Beauty Red Roses.... **$3.29**

7A50—A close fitting, Chic Little Hat of High Grade Satin Duchess, cleverly combined with lustrous Braid and Paisley Pattern Satin. The new curled quill effect at the front of hat is also a combination of these pretty fabrics and is finished with a Paisley Satin covered button. The curled quill effect is one of the season's prettiest hat trimmings. *Colors:* Black, old rose, navy or white with Paisley; or, all black .. **$2.49**

7A46—Handsome Dress Hat with Two Full Head 18-inch Ostrich Plumes. The flues of the feathers are long and wide. The brim, upper and lower, and the side crown are of Superior Quality Durable, yet Fine Braid. Flange and top of crown are of Satin Duchess. The feathers are caught at each side by fine linen roses and droop gracefully over the sides of the brim. *Colors:* All black, all white, or black, Copenhagen, or old rose, with white feather. All with pink linen roses. **$6.49**

7A51—An Exceedingly Becoming Hat of Finest Quality Silk Poplin faced with superior quality Silk Braid. Clusters of Velvet Grapes, varying from the most delicate to the deepest shades of color are combined with Pastel Colored silk leaves to supply the handsome trimming. Rubber stems are entwined and encircle the crown of the hat immediately above the brim. *Colors:* Black, white, Copenhagen, old rose, or bisque, as pictured, or black with white facing........ **$5.49**

7A48—An Excellent Hat for wear with Sport Dresses, or with Shirt Waist and Skirt costumes. The hat is of Extra Fine Quality Peanut Straw. A one-inch flange of red, navy, emerald green or gold imported hemp extends around the brim. Narrower bands of imported hemp in matching colors encircle the crown. At one side is a smart design of Roman Striped Silk Grosgrain ribbon, fastened with a hemp button ornament........................ **$2.25**

FREE DELIVERY OF EVERY PURCHASE

A Stylishly Tailored Suit of All Wool Serge

4A1—Smartly Designed Suit of Excellent Quality All Wool Serge. Lined throughout with figured Sateen. Faultless in every detail. Mannish collar has notched revers and white Silk Repp overlay. Coat has gathers in back, outlined by stitching, below which section it falls in side plaits. Patch pockets have rows of stitching and pearl button trimming. Carefully cut skirt stitched to hip depth on side gores, below which point it falls in graceful plaits. *Colors:* Navy, Copenhagen, mustard or black. *Sizes:* 32 to 46 bust; 40 inch skirt with 3 inch basted hem............... **$13.98**

Handsome Suit for Dress Wear

4A2—Exceptional Value All Wool Poplin Suit. Cleverly fashioned and embodying the latest style details. Lined throughout with soft finished Satin. Novelly cut collar, trimmed with covered buttons and stitching. Ball buttons trim the new double belt, one section of which fastens the "throw-tie" way. Stitching and buttons trim the pockets and cuffs. Double belt at back. Side gores of the skirt are stitched on all seams to hip depth and there released fall in plaits to the hem. Slight gathers at the back beneath the double belt. *Colors:* Navy, apple green, mustard or black. *Sizes:* 32 to 46 bust; 40 inch skirt with 3 inch basted hem................................ **$18.98**

New Style All Wool Jersey Sport Suit

4A3—Superb All Wool Jersey Norfolk Suit. Both front and back, the coat is stitched in plaits from yoke to belt and falls in side plaits below. Collar, "throw-tie" belt and patch pockets embroidered in colors. Cuffs of the material with inverted points, button trimmed. Plain skirt with slashed pockets on each side. Belt of the Jersey cut in yoke effect at the front and button trimmed. Gathers at back eliminate dragging over the hips. *Colors:* Old gold, rose, green, crushed raspberry. *Sizes:* 32 to 46 bust; 40 inch skirt with 3 inch basted hem...... **$21.98**

4A1 $13.98

4A2 $18.98   **4A3 $21.98**

Smartly Tailored Suits for Women

Samples of these Perry-Dame Suit Materials will be sent you gladly, FREE.

4A4—A Handsome Dress Suit of All Wool Velour. Extreme care is evidenced in every detail of its making. The hip and breast pockets are outlined by rows of stitching and fastened with smoked pearl buttons. Stitching also simulates cuffs on the button-trimmed sleeves. The side back seams are also defined by four rows of stitching, a new and pleasing style detail. The deep collar is stitched to match and made in one with the revers. The "throw-tie" belt at waist is another new feature. The deftly tailored skirt is made with slight gathers and buttoned pockets on the side gores, which are finished with a sectional belt at the waist. The back and front panels are stitched to yoke depth and there released to fall in inverted plaits to the hem. *Colors:* Old gold, apple green, rose or navy. *Sizes:* 32 to 46 bust measure.......... **$19.98**

How to Order Your Right Size Suit

Women's Suits come in 32 to 46 bust measure. The skirt length is 40 inches with a deep basted hem for easy adjustment. Send us your bust measure and your waist measure, and we will send you your right size. You may, if you like, also send us your hip measure as an additional guide.

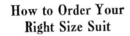

4A5
$16⁹⁸
ALL WOOL
SERGE

4A4
$19⁹⁸
ALL WOOL
VELOUR

4A5—Beautiful, Well-made Suit of Finest Quality All Wool Serge. Lined throughout with Paisley Silk in compliance with the universal demand for this effective material. Pleasing length of line is secured for the back of coat through the three box plaits which extend from the neck to the hem. From below the novelly shaped yoke in front, similar plaits are stitched in folds and terminate at the belt. The collar and revers are cut in one and supplemented by an overlay of picot-edged white broadcloth, embroidered with beads and run with narrow silk soutache braid. The deep pointed patch pockets are trimmed with novelty buttons similar to those which form the closing. The skirt is a smart, plain tailored model, depending for its fulness upon the graceful flare allowed in its cutting and the inverted plaits which fall from below the yoke at the side front and side back gores. The small patch pockets are neatly finished in slashed effect. *Colors:* Navy, black or Copenhagen. *Sizes:* 32 to 46 bust measure.......... **$16.98**

Cleverly Designed Suits for Women

4A7—Handsomely Tailored Suit of Superior Quality All Wool Poplin. Carefully lined throughout with figured silk poplin. The deep square collar has a gracefully rounded overlay of scallop-edged broadcloth, outlined with a double row of stitching. A box plait extends down the center of the back from shoulders to hem. The applied box plaits on the side, both front and back, curve in and form the very unusual "Cavalier" patch pockets. These pockets are trimmed with tiny self-covered buttons, similar to those which trim the sleeves with their slight gathers at the elbow. The smart, plain skirt is finished with a button-trimmed belt and has two conveniently roomy patch pockets. Side front closing. Firmly stitched inside belt. *Colors:* Apple green, mustard, navy or black. *Sizes:* 32 to 46 inches bust measure..................... **$20.98**

4A7
$20⁹⁸
ALL WOOL
POPLIN

4A6
$15⁹⁸
SILK POPLIN

4A6—Dressy Suit of High Lustre Silk Poplin, with a percentage of cotton which adds strength to its wearing qualities. Self-lined throughout. The deep square collar is most unusual in design. It is of novelty striped silk poplin, outlined all around with a turned-back fold of the material and trimmed with covered buttons. The cuffs are treated in a similar manner. Slight gathers beneath the neat belt procure necessary fulness. The unusual patch pockets which are a style feature of this coat have a button fastening. Slight gathers beneath the stitched belt at back of skirt achieve desirable grace and width. *Colors:* Navy, apple green, mustard, Copenhagen or rose. *Sizes:* 32 to 46 inches bust measure...... **$15.98**

Three Serviceable Suits for General Wear

4A8—Smartly Designed Suit of Novelty Black and White Plaid Mixture. Slightly flared coat lined throughout with figured sateen. Stitched belt trimmed with bone buttons. Similar buttons form the closing. They are again used with a fold of matching colored silk repp to trim the chic patch pockets. Square collar, with notched revers, completed with a colored silk repp overlay to harmonize. The skirt is plain in front. Slight gathers beneath the back yoke, which extends over the hips in deep pointed button-trimmed tabs. *Sizes: 32 to 46 bust....* **$11.98**

4A9
$7.48
RATINE

4A8
$11.98
NOVELTY
MIXTURE

4A10
$15.98
ALL WOOL
SERGE

4A9—Norfolk Style Suit of Finest Quality Ratiné. Three deep plaits are stitched from below the front yoke to belt. The back is slightly gathered, the flare of the lower portion being caught by the button-trimmed belt at waist. The slashed pockets are finished with a button-trimmed tab of the ratiné. Turned-back cuffs complete the sleeves. The collar is made of contrasting colored ratiné, outlined with bands of the material at either side. The skirt is a plain tailored model, trimmed with patch pockets to match the coat. The trim fitting belt fits smoothly over the slight gathers at the back. In front it is cut in a deep point. *Colors:* Copenhagen, tan or white. *Sizes: 32 to 46 bust measure.* This is an excellent suit, especially well adapted for Spring and Summer wear.. **$7.48**

A New Model All Wool Serge Suit

4A10—Superior Tailoring Characterizes this Suit of Finest Quality All Wool Serge. The coat is full Seco Silk lined throughout and fitted with underarm shields. Heavy Faille silk overlay greatly enhances the beauty of the fancy stitched collar. The sleeves and pouch pockets are stitched in novel outline and trimmed with buttons. The belt is stitched at the back and also at the ends to match the collar. The front of the well flared skirt is plainly tailored while at the back, beneath the belt, slight gathers insure a smooth fit. One of the season's newest belted flare models which has met with universal approval. *Colors:* Black, navy or Copenhagen. *Sizes: 32 to 46 bust measure...* **$15.98**

Samples of these Perry-Dame Suit materials will be sent you gladly, FREE.

4A12 $14.98 All Wool Serge

4A11 $16.50 All Wool Serge

4A13 $19.98 All Wool Poplin

4A12—Service Giving Suit of Fine All Wool Serge. Carefully tailored on most becoming lines. Lined throughout with Figured Sateen. The square collar of the material has notched revers and an overlay of striped silk poplin. The lower portion of the coat is made in panel effect both front and back. Stitched belt at waist confines the fulness. The wide patch pockets and the sleeves are trimmed with buttons. The skirt is a smooth fitting, plain tailored model, made with a graduated flare. Convenient side front closing. *Colors:* Navy, mustard, Copenhagen or black. *Sizes:* 32 to 46 bust measure. An extremely good value suit cut in the latest fashion.... **$14.98**

4A11—Trim Looking Dress Suit of Very Superior All Wool Serge. Lined to the waist with Paisley Pattern Satin, which also furnishes the sleeve lining. The coat is prettily box-plaited all around in the latest mode. At the belt the plaits are released and fall in graceful folds. The deep collar has an overlay of fine Silk Faille, stitched in contrasting color. The closing may be continued to the throat by buttons on the yoke, or left open. Below the yoke the coat is closed by snap fasteners, presenting a neat appearance. Cleverly fashioned skirt has long tabs of the material applied from the belt to hip depth on the side seams. Below this point a box plait has been adroitly inserted. *Colors:* Black or navy. *Sizes:* 32 to 46 bust **16.50**

4A13—A Handsome Suit of Excellent Quality All Wool Poplin. Carefully made. Lined throughout with figured silk poplin. The button-trimmed collar of the material has notched revers; and a stitched White Broadcloth Collar with scalloped edge. Front and back of coat display a panel, at either side of which three side plaits are introduced below the belt to give necessary fulness. Patch pockets lined with silk and suspended from beneath the belt in accord with the latest vogue. The sleeves have straight-edged white broadcloth cuffs with two rows of stitching to match the collar. The skirt is in the latest style, the side gores falling in inverted plaits below the hips. *Colors:* Mustard, apple green, navy or black. *Sizes:* 32 to 46 bust. **$19.98**

4A16—An Ideal Spring and Summer Suit of Gray and White or Black and White Woven Shepherd Check. Figured sateen supplies the lining. The square collar of the material is enhanced by a gracefully rounded collar of silk poplin. The stitched cuffs are trimmed with bone buttons similar to those which achieve the closing. The "throw-tie" belt passes through loops at the waist and so adjusts the fulness. The applied pockets are made with a button fastening. The coat may be worn open, as pictured, or buttoned close to the throat, as occasion requires. The skirt is an exceedingly smart plain tailored model, being trimmed with patch pockets, similar to those which adorn the coat. Slight gathers appear beneath the button-trimmed belt at back of skirt. *Sizes:* 32 to 46 bust measure..... **$10.98**

4A17—Well-made Suit of Wool and Cotton Serge. Lined throughout with fancy sateen. The square collar is trimmed with bone buttons and made with an insert of heavy silk repp. Button-trimmed cuffs, sectional belt and back panel. Smart patch pockets fasten with large buttons. Slight gathers beneath belt at back insure the fit and graceful flare of the well tailored skirt. *Colors:* Navy or black. *Sizes:* 32 to 46 bust..... **$9.98**

4A17
$9 98
SERGE

4A14—Cleverly Designed Suit of Superior All Wool Poplin. Stitching is in great demand this season on all the latest model suits. Here it is seen in rows on the collar, revers, cuffs, belt, and patch pockets. The belt is also trimmed with small pearl buckles, and tassel ends. The slight gathers of the side and front seams are accentuated at the back to give pleasing fulness. The coat lining is of figured sateen, in a very pretty pattern. The skirt is a plain tailored model, expert tailoring being apparent in every line. Stitched belt at waist and side front closing. *Colors:* Navy, green, gold or black, stitched in contrasting shades. *Sizes:* 32 to 46 bust measure. An exceptional suit at a very reasonable price........ **$15.98**

4A14
$15 98
ALL WOOL POPLIN

4A15
$6 48
BEACH CLOTH

4A16
$10 98
FANCY CHECK

4A15—A Serviceable, Cool and Comfortable Summer Suit of Wear-resisting Beach Cloth. It sheds the dust readily and may be laundered without the slightest hesitancy. The unlined coat is made with the square collar and revers in one. Button-trimmed points appear on the neat belt which adjusts the fulness. The patch pockets are of very unusual design, those at the bottom of the coat being suspended from the breast pockets, which are trimmed with pearl buttons. A shallow yoke is formed at the back of the plain tailored skirt by means of a stitched band of the beach cloth. In natural color only. *Sizes:* 32 to 46 bust measure...... **$6.48**

Particularly Becoming Suits for Women

4A19—Cleverly Tailored Suit of Finest Quality All Wool Poplin. Lined throughout with high grade Peau de Cygne, and fitted with underarm shields. From beneath the well fitting yoke both front and back tiny box plaits extend to the belt. The fashionable flared coat falls with a gradual increase in width from beneath the stitched belt at waist. The button-trimmed tabs of the material are lined with Peau de Cygne, and completed with tiny slashed pockets. The overlay on the well shaped square collar is of heavy silk poplin to harmonize. The skirt is made with a panel back, stitched to hip depth and then released. The side back gores are very slightly gathered beneath a simulated yoke. *Colors:* Navy, black, apple green or mustard. *Sizes:* 32 to 46 bust measure................... **$22.98**

Samples of Perry-Dame Suit materials will be sent you gladly, FREE.

4A18—Suit of Superior Quality All Wool Poplin. The collar with its notched revers has an overlay of white silk repp. Gold threads combine with silk to trim the "throw-tie" belt, which terminates in pretty tassels. Beneath the belt the coat falls in box plaits. Silk and gold threads are used to simulate cuffs on the slightly flared sleeves. Art Sateen lining in a dainty floral design extends to the waist. The plain tailored skirt has a belt in back beneath which fall slight gathers. *Colors:* Copenhagen, apple green, mustard, navy or black. *Sizes:* 32 to 46 bust..... **$15.98**

4A20
$12.98
ALL WOOL SERGE

4A19
$22.98
ALL WOOL POPLIN

4A20—Trim appearing Suit of High Grade All Wool Serge cut on mannish lines. Full sateen lined. The collar is cut in novel outline and completed with a piqué detachable overlay. The coat flares prettily from beneath the belt. Bone buttons trim the belt, sleeves, back of coat and fold on the slashed pockets. Smart plain tailored skirt. Slight shirrings beneath back belt. *Colors:* Copenhagen, mustard, navy or black. *Sizes:* 32 to 46 bust. **$12.98**

4A18
$15.98
ALL WOOL POPLIN

Youthful Suits for Misses and Small Women

How to Order Your Right Size Suit

Misses' Suits come in sizes 14 to 20 years, in accordance with the following schedule:
14 yrs., bust 32 ins., skirt 31 ins.
16 yrs., bust 34 ins., skirt 33 ins.
18 yrs., bust 36 ins., skirt 35 ins.
20 yrs., bust 38 ins., skirt 37 ins.
Deep basted hem for easy adjustment.

4A102
$12⁹⁸
ALL WOOL SERGE

4A102—Suit of Finely Woven All Wool Serge. The flare coat is lined with sateen and confined by the belt at waist. Beneath belt slight gathers gain fulness for the back. Square collar with an overlay of silk poplin. Stitching is seen on the collar, cuffs, pockets and side plaits which fall beneath the belt. The plain skirt has an overlapping front seam. The back is made with a sectional belt, and has slight gathers. *Colors:* Black, navy, mustard or Copenhagen. *Sizes:* 14 to 20 years..... **$12.98**

4A101
$15⁷⁵
ALL WOOL POPLIN

4A101—Suit of Superior Quality All Wool Poplin. Flare coat lined with Seco Silk, confined at waist by the "throw-tie" belt. The deep square collar has a white silk poplin overlay. The ends of the belt are finished with straight rows of stitching to match sleeve trimming. The lower patch pockets are suspended from the breast pockets. Stitched designs trim the collar and also the belt in back. Plain tailored skirt, out with graceful flare, finished at the front with an overlapping seam and with a button-trimmed belt at back. *Colors:* Navy, black, apple green or mustard. *Sizes:* 14 to 20 years............ **$15.75**

4A103—A Cleverly Fashioned Suit of Good Quality Woven Check. The sectional belt extends from either side of the smooth, plain back. Slight gathers at the waist give requisite fulness to the front of coat. Gathered pouch pockets are trimmed with buttons and tabs of the material. The white piqué collar is trimmed with buttons and sets smoothly over the collar of the material which has deep pointed revers. Lined throughout with flowered sateen. The neatly finished skirt is cut perfectly plain, both back and front, and fastens invisibly at one side. *Colors:* Black and white check only. *Sizes:* 14 to 20 years.. **$9.98**

4A103
$9⁴⁸
SHEPHERD CHECK

Stylish Suits Especially Designed for Misses and Small Women

4A104—Carefully Tailored Suit of Finest Quality All Wool Velour. The belted flare coat is one of the season's most popular models. The collar, cuffs, patch pockets and edge of coat display rows of contrasting colored stitching, a neat and pleasing mode of ornamentation. In back the material is stitched to yoke depth and falls in inverted plaits. The belt at back terminates at either side of front, where it is fastened to the box plait with a large pearl button. The skirt is a fashionable plain tailored model, made with very slight gathers beneath the belt in back. *Colors:* Apple green, mustard, navy or old rose. *Sizes:* 14 to 20 years.................**$18.98**

4A106 S648 KOOL CLOTH

4A104 $1898 ALL WOOL VELOUR

4A105 $1198 ALL WOOL SERGE

Samples of these Perry-Dame Suit Materials will be sent you gladly, FREE.

4A105—Chic Little Suit of All Wool Serge of very fine grade. Lined throughout with figured sateen. The back is made with box plaits which extend from beneath yoke in Norfolk style. Button-trimmed belt passes through loops on the patch pockets which are also trimmed with buttons. Collar has notched revers and is supplemented by an overlay of Silk Poplin which also supplies the cuffs. The well-cut skirt is plain in front and has slight gathers beneath the sectional belt at the back. *Colors:* Navy, black or mustard. *Sizes:* 14 to 20 years. **$11.98**

4A106—Charming Summer Suit of Kool Cloth —a specially well-named material as it is both cool and comfortable. The coat is one of the new belted flare models, cut on mannish lines and finished with patch pockets. Neatly stitched collar with notched revers. Sleeves have turned-back cuffs of the material. The "throw-tie" belt is trimmed at back with fine pearl buttons, similar to those which effect the closing. The skirt is cut perfectly plain in front. At the back very scant gathers are introduced beneath the shallow yoke. *Colors:* Light tan only. *Sizes:* 14 to 20 years....**$6.48**

Newest Gloves for Spring and Summer Wear

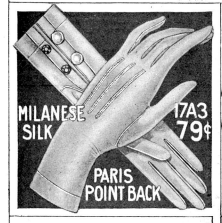

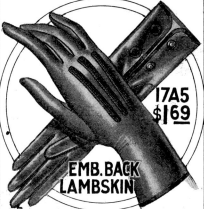

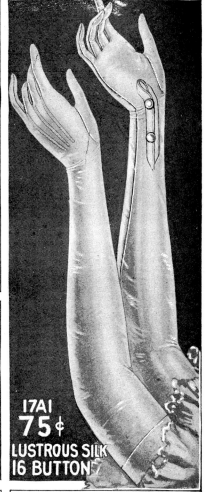

MILANESE SILK **17A3 79¢** **PARIS POINT BACK**

17A5 $1.69 **EMB. BACK LAMBSKIN**

17A1 75¢ LUSTROUS SILK 16 BUTTON

17A3—High-grade Milanese Silk Gloves, made with Paris Point stitching on the back in self color. The carefully stitched fingers are finished with double tips to insure their durability. *Colors:* Black or white. *Sizes:* 6 to 8...........**.79**

17A5—Soft and Pliable Gloves of Excellent Quality Lambskin with embroidered backs. French seamed throughout. *Colors:* White with black or black with white stitching. *Sizes:* 6 to 8.......................**$1.69**

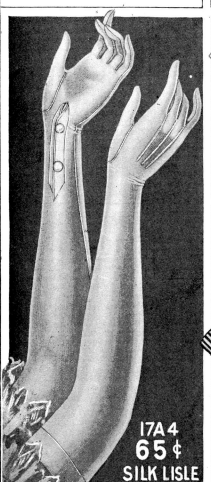

EMB. BACK **17A2 $1.49** **WASHABLE DOE SKIN**

17A2—Washable Gloves of Fine White Doeskin, very well suited for Summer wear as they may be cleansed whenever required. Firmly stitched outseams. *Colors:* White with black embroidered backs. *Sizes:* 6 to 8...................**$1.49**

17A1—16-Button Length Gloves of Cool and Comfortable Tricot Silk, especially well adapted for Summer wear. The gloves are cut long enough to reach well above the elbow. Neat stitching in self color outlines the backs. Durability is insured by the double finger tips. *Colors:* Black or white. *Sizes:* 6 to 8......................**.75**

17A6 $1.29 **HEAVY MILANESE SILK** **LATEST STYLE IDEA**

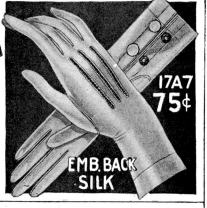

17A4 65¢ SILK LISLE

17A7 75¢ **EMB. BACK SILK**

17A4—Well-made Silk Lisle Gloves in either black or white, stitched in self color. Cut sufficiently long to reach well above the elbow. They may be had in black or white. *Sizes:* 6 to 8...............**.65**

17A6—Gloves of Heavy Milanese Silk, neatly embroidered in black and white and finished with a black and white striped silk cuff, one of the newest style gloves. Double finger tips. *Colors:* White or black trimmed as described. *Sizes:* 6 to 8..........**$1.29**

17A7—Easily Laundered Gloves of Cool and Comfortable Tricot Silk. In white embroidered with black, or black embroidered with white stitching. The double finger tips increase their wearing qualities. *Sizes:* 6 to 8.......................**.75**

Women's Gloves of Remarkable Value

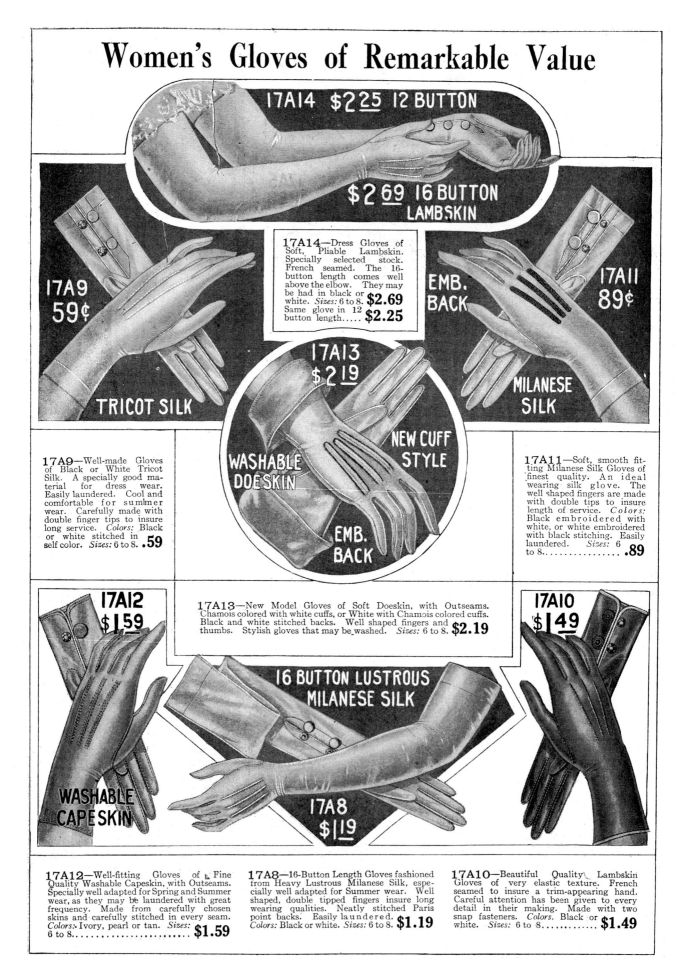

17A14 $2.25 12 BUTTON

$2.69 16 BUTTON LAMBSKIN

17A9 59¢

TRICOT SILK

17A14—Dress Gloves of Soft, Pliable Lambskin. Specially selected stock. French seamed. The 16-button length comes well above the elbow. They may be had in black or white. *Sizes:* 6 to 8. **$2.69** Same glove in 12 button length..... **$2.25**

EMB. BACK

17A11 89¢

MILANESE SILK

17A13 $2.19

WASHABLE DOESKIN

NEW CUFF STYLE

EMB. BACK

17A9—Well-made Gloves of Black or White Tricot Silk. A specially good material for dress wear. Easily laundered. Cool and comfortable for summer wear. Carefully made with double finger tips to insure long service. *Colors:* Black or white stitched in self color. *Sizes:* 6 to 8. **.59**

17A11—Soft, smooth fitting Milanese Silk Gloves of finest quality. An ideal wearing silk glove. The well shaped fingers are made with double tips to insure length of service. *Colors:* Black embroidered with white, or white embroidered with black stitching. Easily laundered. *Sizes:* 6 to 8................ **.89**

17A12 $1.59

WASHABLE CAPESKIN

17A13—New Model Gloves of Soft Doeskin, with Outseams. Chamois colored with white cuffs, or White with Chamois colored cuffs. Black and white stitched backs. Well shaped fingers and thumbs. Stylish gloves that may be washed. *Sizes:* 6 to 8. **$2.19**

16 BUTTON LUSTROUS MILANESE SILK

17A8 $1.19

17A10 $1.49

17A12—Well-fitting Gloves of Fine Quality Washable Capeskin, with Outseams. Specially well adapted for Spring and Summer wear, as they may be laundered with great frequency. Made from carefully chosen skins and carefully stitched in every seam. *Colors:* Ivory, pearl or tan. *Sizes:* 6 to 8........................ **$1.59**

17A8—16-Button Length Gloves fashioned from Heavy Lustrous Milanese Silk, especially well adapted for Summer wear. Well shaped, double tipped fingers insure long wearing qualities. Neatly stitched Paris point backs. Easily laundered. *Colors:* Black or white. *Sizes:* 6 to 8. **$1.19**

17A10—Beautiful Quality Lambskin Gloves of very elastic texture. French seamed to insure a trim-appearing hand. Careful attention has been given to every detail in their making. Made with two snap fasteners. *Colors:* Black or white. *Sizes:* 6 to 8............ **$1.49**

Specially Designed Corsets for Every Figure

HOW TO ORDER YOUR RIGHT SIZE CORSET. Order your corset by size, not by waist measure. The correct size of a regular corset, also reducing and maternity models is three inches less than your waist measure, taken over your dress. Topless Corsets and Misses' Corset Waists should be ordered two inches smaller than your waist measure, taken over your dress. Front lacing corsets should be ordered one inch smaller than your waist measure, taken over your dress.

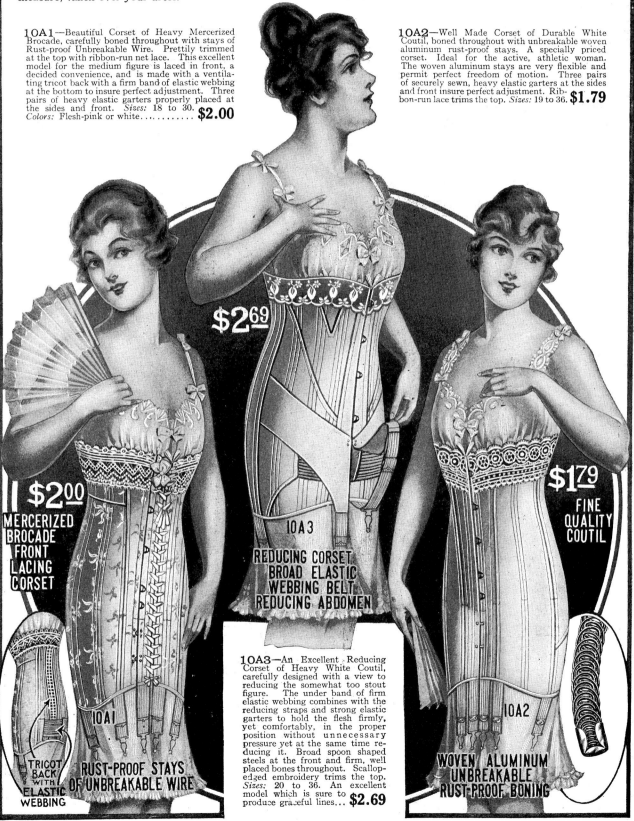

10A1—Beautiful Corset of Heavy Mercerized Brocade, carefully boned throughout with stays of Rust-proof Unbreakable Wire. Prettily trimmed at the top with ribbon-run net lace. This excellent model for the medium figure is laced in front, a decided convenience, and is made with a ventilating tricot back with a firm band of elastic webbing at the bottom to insure perfect adjustment. Three pairs of heavy elastic garters properly placed at the sides and front. *Sizes:* 18 to 30. *Colors:* Flesh-pink or white............ **$2.00**

10A2—Well Made Corset of Durable White Coutil, boned throughout with unbreakable woven aluminum rust-proof stays. A specially priced corset. Ideal for the active, athletic woman. The woven aluminum stays are very flexible and permit perfect freedom of motion. Three pairs of securely sewn, heavy elastic garters at the sides and front insure perfect adjustment. Ribbon-run lace trims the top. *Sizes:* 19 to 36. **$1.79**

$2⁶⁹

$2⁰⁰
MERCERIZED BROCADE FRONT LACING CORSET

10A3
REDUCING CORSET BROAD ELASTIC WEBBING BELT REDUCING ABDOMEN

$1⁷⁹
FINE QUALITY COUTIL

10A1

TRICOT BACK WITH ELASTIC WEBBING

RUST-PROOF STAYS OF UNBREAKABLE WIRE

10A3—An Excellent Reducing Corset of Heavy White Coutil, carefully designed with a view to reducing the somewhat too stout figure. The under band of firm elastic webbing combines with the reducing straps and strong elastic garters to hold the flesh firmly, yet comfortably, in the proper position without unnecessary pressure yet at the same time reducing it. Broad spoon shaped steels at the front and firm, well placed bones throughout. Scalloped-edged embroidery trims the top. *Sizes:* 20 to 36. An excellent model which is sure to produce graceful lines... **$2.69**

10A2

WOVEN ALUMINUM UNBREAKABLE RUST-PROOF BONING

Women's Corsets

Read How to Order Correct Size Corset on Page 87.

10A6—Fine White Coutil Corset, specially designed for short stout figures. Lace-trimmed top. No bulging of the flesh above the top to mar the appearance of the dress. Heavily boned throughout and fitted with two pairs of heavy elastic webbing garters. *Sizes:* 19 to 36. White only......... **$1.19**

10A5—A Well-made Front-laced Corset with ventilating tricot back and elastic insert. Durable duplex boning throughout. Three pairs of firm elastic webbing garters. An excellent model, which contributes long, graceful lines to the wearer. *Sizes:* 18 to 30. White only.............. **$1.69**

IO A 5 $1.69

FASHIONABLE FRONT LACING MODEL

SPECIALLY DESIGNED FOR SHORT STOUT FIGURES

IOA6 $1.19

10A4—Handsome Lace-trimmed Brocade Reducing Corset. Made with adjustable abdominal straps and strong front steels. Three sets of garters. *Colors:* Flesh-pink or white. *Sizes:* 20 to 36... **$2.00**

10A9—Well-proportioned Corset of Finest Mercerized Brocade. Carefully boned and designed to confine the figure without unpleasantly binding it. *Sizes:* 19 to 30. *Colors:* White or flesh-pink. Exceptionally low priced **$1.29**

10A8—Front Laced 10-inch Grecian Girdle. The sides are of broad bands of heavy elastic webbing securely joined to a boned coutil section at the back. Two pairs of firm garters hold the corset securely in position. *Sizes:* 19 to 30. *Colors:* White or flesh-pink **$1.89**

IOA7 $2.49

FRONT LACING ELASTIC GIRDLE

VENTILATING TRICOT BACK WITH ELASTIC INSERT

MERCERIZED BROCADE BONED TO CORRECT DEPTH

IO A 9 $1.29

IOA8 $1.89

FRONT LACING CORSET WITH STRONG ELASTIC WEBBING GIVING COMFORT AND A PERFECT FIGURE

10A7—Handsome Front Lacing Corset of Heavy Elastic Webbing. Specially designed for outdoor sport wear. The side gores are carefully stitched to the back of coutil, with its broad flexible bones. Perfect comfort, freedom of motion and a graceful figure are assured. Two pairs of heavy elastic garters offer secure adjustment. *Sizes:* 19 to 30. *Colors:* Flesh-pink or white.. **$2.49**

Women's Corsets

10A12—Cool, Comfortable Corset of Ventilating Mesh, light but very firmly woven. The strong front steel and flexible boning at the sides and back insure good wearing qualities. Especially designed for medium figures. *Sizes:* 18 to 30. White only..........**.75**

10A14—Well Made Corset intended especially for the slender figure. Made of medium weight white coutil and boned throughout with non-rustable aluminized wires. Neatly finished at the top with embroidery and fitted with two pairs of garters. *Sizes:* 18 to 26.......**.79**

COUTIL
NON-RUSTABLE
WIRE

79c
10A14

10A12
75c

VENTILATING
MESH
FLEXIBLE
BONING
STRONG
FRONT
STEELS

10A11
$2.00

REDUCING
CORSET

BROAD
FRONT
STEELS

REINFORCED
REDUCING
STRAPS

STRONG
ELASTIC
WEBBING
FOR
COMFORT

10A10
$2.00

ELASTIC
TOP

10A13
$1.00
NO
STEELS
OVER
HIPS

10A10—Comfortable Corset of High Grade Coutil made with strong elastic webbing at the top and bottom, insuring easy fit and long straight lines. The elastic sections at the top and bottom prevent unsightly bulging. Fitted with heavy front and back steels and flexible bones. An excellent model for the average figure. *Sizes:* 20 to 30. White only.....**$2.00**

ELASTIC WEBBING
GIVING PERFECTLY
STRAIGHT LINES

10A11—An Excellent Reducing Corset of Heavy Coutil, made with broad front steel and reinforced reducing straps, gently and firmly reducing the abdomen. The garters are of heavy elastic webbing and hold the corset firmly in the proper position. The boning throughout is very firm yet flexible. Deep ribbon-run lace, finished with a satin rosette, trims the top. *Sizes:* 20 to 36. White only.....**$2.00**

10A13—Excellent Corset of Medium Weight Coutil. The low bust with its elastic top and the absence of steels over the hips insure perfect comfort and freedom of motion. Strong front and back steels, but very flexible boning at the side front and side back gores. The laced portion at the front and the garters of firm elastic insure perfect adjustment. Intended for medium figures. *Sizes:* 18 to 26. White only.....**$1.00**

10A19—Girl's Corset Waist with light, flexible boning. Designed to hold the immature figure within trim lines, without in any way binding it. Tape sewn bone buttons form the front closing. Similar buttons are placed at the sides for convenience in fastening the under garments. *Sizes:* 18 to 30. White only. A corset waist every girl should have.......... **.79**

10A15—Maternity and Nursing Corset with light, flexible boning. The extra lacings at the sides and front permit of easy adjustment. The bust is made with an open section for convenience in nursing and here the closing is effected by means of secure snap fasteners. Two pairs of elastic garters. An excellent model designed with a view to comfort. *Sizes:* 20 to 36. White only.......... **$1.69**

10A19
79c
GIRL'S
CORSET WAIST
LIGHT
FLEXIBLE
BONING

10A15
$1.69
MATERNITY
NURSING
CORSET
FLEXIBLE
BONING

10A17
$1.19
REDUCING
CORSET
ADJUSTABLE
ABDOMINAL
STRAPS

10A17—Reducing Corset of Strong Coutil, especially designed for stout figures. Made with broad front steels and adjustable abdominal straps, which hold the abdomen in place without unnecessary pressure. Three pairs of heavy elastic webbing garters hold the corset securely in position. The top is trimmed with ribbon run lace. White only. *Sizes:* 19 to 36....... **$1.19**

10A16—Durable White Coutil Corset. A fashionable front laced model. Designed particularly for medium figures. The well placed bones and steels extend to correct depth and produce a gracefully rounded, slender figure. Carefully sewn garters insure perfect adjustment. White only. *Sizes:* 18 to 30....... **$1.10**

10A16
FRONT
LACING
CORSET
GIVING
GRACEFUL
AND FASHIONABLE LINES
$1.10

See How to
Order Corsets
on Page 87.

10A18
$1.25
COUTIL
CORSET
FIRM
FLEXIBLE
BONING
WITH
STRONG
FRONT
STEELS

10A18—A Good Corset of firm White Coutil, for the medium and average figure. Made with flexible aluminum wire warranted not to rust, and strong front spoon-shaped steels. Three pairs of strong elastic garters secure comfortable adjustment of the skirt portion. White only. *Sizes:* 19 to 36....... **$1.25**

PERRY·DAME·QUALITY·SHOES
for WOMEN MISSES and CHILDREN

"QUALITY SHOES" means something—it means not ordinary shoes but BETTER SHOES.

BETTER AND MORE BEAUTIFUL IN STYLE.
BETTER IN LASTING WEARING QUALITIES.
BETTER VALUE FOR YOUR DOLLARS.

We want you for a REGULAR SHOE CUSTOMER and we ask you to try a pair of PERRY-DAME QUALITY SHOES. If you do, you will wear them always—they will give PERFECT SHOE SATISFACTION. THIS WE GUARANTEE.

How to Order Your Right Size Shoe

It is a very simple matter to get perfect-fitting Shoes from Perry, Dame & Co. Just order by the size and width you usually wear, or if you wish, send us a pencil outline of your stockinged foot drawn with the foot pressed down on a piece of paper laid flat on the floor, as shown in the picture here.
When ordering Children's Shoes, be sure to order them large enough, as children's feet grow rapidly.

6A5—Carefully made "Cinderella" Pump of High Grade Patent Leather. Smart two-button fancy cut-out strap over the instep. Jet ornament trims the vamp. Medium weight sole. Slightly recede toe. Concave Cuban heel. *Sizes:* 2½ to 8. Widths C, D and E.... **$2.69**

6A2—Finely Arched Patent Leather Arrow Pump, perforated as illustrated. Smart recede toe, Louis heel and dress weight sole. The non-slip ooze lining prevents chafing at the heel. A desirable selection for dress wear. *Size:* 2½ to 7. Widths C, D and E...... **$3.15**

6A3—Well Made Gun Metal Leather Colonial Pump with new style white kid inlay on tongue, as pictured. Smartly curved Louis heel. Smart recede toe. The non-slip ooze lining prevents slipping. *Sizes:* 2½ to 7. Widths C, D and E.. **$3.15**

6A3

6A5

6A2

INSPECTED
PERFECT
SKIN

Women's Fashionable Shoes

6A14—"Priscilla" Pump of Black Patent Leather. Fancy metal ornament on vamp and on the three cut-out straps over the instep. Spool heel. Slightly recede toe. Sizes: 2½ to 8. Widths, C, D and E. A smart looking pump, specially adapted for dress wear.................... **$2.69**

6A4—"Mary Jane" Ankle Strap Patent Leather Pump, trimmed with a tailored bow on vamp. Wide toe and military heel. Sizes: 2½ to 8. Widths, C, D and E...... **$2.25**

6A7—Black Cabretta Kid "Mary Jane" Pump. Tailored bow on vamp. Wide toe and military heel. Sizes: 2½ to 8. Widths, C, D and E. Here is found the acme of foot comfort. **$1.89**

6A1—Patent Leather Colonial Pump, with jet metal buckle, Colonial tongue. Smart recede toe. Louis heel. Non-slip lining. Sizes: 2½ to 8, Widths, C, D and E............. **$2.75**

6A13—Gun Metal Colonial Pump. Dull metal buckle. Smart recede toe and spool heel. Non-slipping lining. Sizes: 2½ to 8. Widths, C, D and E... **$2.59**

6A11—The "Peggy" Pump of superior grade Patent Leather with dull kid inlay and metal ornament on vamp. Stylish toe. Spool heel. Non-slip lining. Sizes: 2½ to 8. Widths, C, D and E..................... **$2.50**

6A6—Fine Black Kid two-button cut out Pump with spool heel. Jet ornament on vamp. Sizes: 2½ to 8. Widths, C, D and E.................... **$2.69**

6A12—Patent Leather four strap Pump. Spool heel. Medium round toe. Jet ornament on vamp. Sizes: 2½ to 8. Widths, C, D and E..... **$2.59**

6A9—9 Strap Roman Sandal. Excellent quality Patent Leather Vamp and dull kid quarter. Slightly recede toe. Spool heel. Reinforced straps. Sizes: 2½ to 7. Widths, C, D and E. **$2.98**

6A10—High Cut Laced Shoe. Fine Quality Patent Leather. Soft dull black kid top with patent leather slashed collar. Smart recede toe. Louis heel. Sizes: 2½ to 8. Widths, C, D and E. **$3.98**

6A8—The "Promenade." A fashionable high cut laced Boot of fine quality soft black Vici Kid. Smart recede toe. Louis heel. Sizes: 2½ to 8. Widths, C, D and E...... **$3.98**

Smart Shoes for Dress Wear

6A25—Two Strap Patent Leather Pump. Medium round toe. Spool heel. Sizes: 2½ to 8. Widths C, D and E..... **$2.49**

6A19—Fashionable High Cut Laced Black and White Shoe. Black kid vamp and collar, perforated as shown. Soft white kid top. Smart recede toe. Louis heel. Sizes: 2½ to 7. Widths C, D and E........ **$4.50**

6A17—Fancy Cross Strap Patent Leather Pump. Jet ornament on vamp. Non-slip lining. Smart recede toe. Spool heel. Sizes: 2½ to 8. Widths C, D and E..................... **$2.65**

6A15—Soft Black Kid Cross Strap Slipper. Hand Turned Sole. Recede toe. Beaded straps and vamp. Sizes: 2½ to 7. Widths C, D and E..... **$3.50**

6A206—Patent "Mary Jane" Ankle Strap Colonial Pump. Natural Foot Shape Last. Sizes: 7 to 8, **$1.49**; 8½ to 11, **$1.75**; 11½ to 2, **$2.25**; 2½ to 6, **$2.49**.

6A205—Patent Leather Cross Strap Pump. Natural Foot Shape Last. Sizes: 7 to 8, **$1.69**; 8½ to 11, **$1.95**; 11½ to 2, **$2.45**; 2½ to 6, **$2.65**.

6A205

6A22—Black Kid Five Bar 2-Button Pump with concave heel and slightly recede toe. Non-slip lining. Sizes: 2½ to 8. Widths, C, D and E.. **$2.75**

6A23—The same style as 6A22, but in Patent Leather............... **$2.75**

6A21—Havana Brown Soft Kid Leather Colonial. Recede toe. Louis heel. Non-slip lining. Sizes: 2½ to 7. Widths C, D and E **$2.98**

6A18—Black and White Kid Colonial. White metal buckle. White kid cutout on top and tongue. Smart recede toe. Louis heel. Sizes: 2½ to 7. Widths C, D and E...... **$3.15**

Stylish High Cut Shoes

6A20—Fashionable High Cut Shoe. Patent Chrome Tanned Vamp and Collar perforated as shown. Soft white kid top. Smart recede toe. Louis heel. Sizes: 2½ to 7. Widths C, D and E. **$4.50**

6A24—Satin Evening Slipper. Satin beaded bow. Satin covered heel. Non-slip lining. Colors: Black, white, pink or light blue. Sizes: 2½ to 7. Widths C, D and E............. **$2.15**

6A16—Patent "Mary Jane" Pump. Guaranteed White Flexible Fibre Sole. White Rubber Heel. Tailored white silk bow. Medium round toe. Sizes: 2½ to 7. Widths C, D and E **$2.69**

High Grade Shoes Embodying Excellence of Material, Workmanship and Design

6A33—Soft black Kid Princess Pump. Jet ornament and neat perforation. Smart recede toe. Louis heel. Non-slip lining. Sizes: 2½ to 8. Widths C, D and E. **$2.98**

6A28—Colonial Pump of Battleship Gray Soft Kid Leather. Oxidized buckle. Non-slip lining. Smart recede toe. Gray finished Louis heels and soles. Sizes: 2½ to 7. Widths C, D and E....... **$2.98**

6A52—Gun Metal Leather Laced Oxford. Medium round toe. Cuban heel. Sizes: 2½ to 8. Widths C, D and E....... **$2.59**

6A39—Low Heeled Patent Leather Colonial Pump. Loop in back stay for detachable strap. High round toe. Non-slip lining. Sizes: 2½ to 8. Widths C, D and E. **$2.59**

6A63—Fashionable High Cut White Sea Island Canvas Laced Boot. Guaranteed Light Tread Rubber Sole. Slightly recede toe. Canvas covered heel with leather top lift. Sizes: 2½ to 7. Widths C, D and E.. **$2.49**

6A30—Gun Metal Leather Walking Shoe. Made on the new "College" Last. Guaranteed fibre sole, will outwear leather. Low rubber heel. Soft dull kid top. Sizes: 2½ to 8. Widths C, D and E.. **$3.75**

6A31—Same style as 6A30 but with patent leather vamp and dull kid top. **$3.75**

FIBRE SOLE

RUBBER HEEL

6A35—All Patent Leather Diamond Pump. Fancy cut out tongue. Non-slip lining. Smart recede toe. Louis heel. Sizes: 2½ to 8. Widths C, D and E................. **$2.98**

6A29—Smart Colonial Pump. Patent Leather Vamp. Brocade quarter. Black metal buckle. Spool heel. Non-slip lining. Medium round toe. Sizes: 2½ to 8. Widths C, D and E..... **$2.25**

6A36—Patent Leather Cross Strap Pump. Low heel. Full round toe. Jet ornament on vamp. Sizes: 2½ to 8. Widths C, D and E. **$2.65**

6A51—Patent Leather Colonial Pump. Soft dull quarter. Oxidized buckle. Non-slip lining. Medium round toe. Concave heel. Sizes: 2½ to 8. Widths C, D and E.. **$2.69**

Barefoot Sandals and Play Oxfords for Boys and Girls

6A204 — Elk Skin Play Oxford. Guaranteed not to rip. Chrome Leather Sole. Sizes: 6 to 8, **$1.25**; 8½ to 11, **$1.45**; 11½ to 2, **$1.69**; 2½ to 5½, **$2.15**.

6A201—White Calfskin Barefoot Sandal with white welt and white Never-rip fibre sole. Sizes: 6 to 8, **$1.19**; 8½ to 11, **$1.35**; 11½ to 2, **$1.60**; 2½ to 5½, **$1.98**.

6A203—Tan Calfskin Play Oxford. Never-rip Chrome sole. Sizes: 6 to 8, **$1.25**; 8½ to 11, **$1.45**; 11½ to 2, **$1.69**; 2½ to 5½, **$2.15**.

6A202—Tan Calfskin Barefoot Sandal with fibre Never-rip sole. Sizes: 6 to 8, **$1.19**; 8½ to 11, **$1.35**; 11½ to 2, **$1.60**; 2½ to 5½, **$1.98**.

6A44—Well Made Gun Metal Leather Sport Oxford. Made on the new "College" last. Guaranteed fibre sole. Low rubber heel. *Sizes: 2½* to 7. Widths C, D and E. **$3.25**

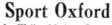

6A45—The "Cleopatra" Patent Leather Pump. Medium round toe. Concave heel. Non-slip lining. *Sizes:* 2½ to 7. Widths C, D and E. **$2.39**

6A40—Patent Leather "Kewpie" Pump. Slightly recede toe. Louis heel. Non-slip lining. *Sizes:* 2½ to 8. Widths C, D and E.. **$2.69**

6A41—Patent Leather 4-Button Oxford. Dull Kid Top. High round toe. Cuban heel. *Sizes:* 2½ to 8. Widths C, D and E............ **$2.59**
6A42—Same style but in Gun Metal Leather Vamp **$2.59**

6A43—Bronze Kid Colonial Pump with cut out instep strap. Bronze covered French heel. Metal ornament on vamp. *Sizes:* 2½ to 7. Widths C, D and E.

$2.98

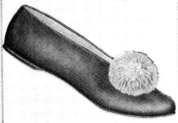

6A38—Dainty Boudoir Slipper in Gold or Silver Leatherette. Quilted lining. Sheepskin sole. Spring heel. *Sizes: 2* to 7.. **.85**

"Mary Jane" Colonial Pump

6A27—Patent Leather "Mary Jane" Colonial Pump. Medium round toe. Cuban heel with rubber top lift. Black metal Colonial buckle. These pumps are made by a process which insures flexibility and comfort. *Sizes:* 2½ to 8. Widths C, D and E.. **$2.50**

6A37—Soft Black Kidskin "Peggy" Pump. Round toe. Military heel. Detachable strap. Flexible sole. *Sizes:* 2½ to 8. Widths C, D and E..... **$2.59**

6A46—High Cut Laced "Parade" Boot of Battleship Gray Soft Kid Leather. Perforated as shown. Smart recede toe. Gray finished Louis heel and sole. *Sizes:* 2½ to 7. Widths C, D and E. **$3.98**

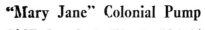

The Blucherette

6A47—The "Blucherette" High Cut Buttoned Shoe. Superb quality Patent Leather Vamp and Dull Kid Top. Recede toe. Louis heel. *Sizes:* 2½ to 7. Widths C, D and E. **$3.50**

6A48—High Cut Laced "Parade" Boot of Havana Brown. Soft Kid Leather. Neatly perforated vamps and tops. Smart recede toe. Louis heel. *Sizes:* 2½ to 7. Widths C, D and E.

$3.98

The Parade Boot

The Parade Boot

Shoes For All Occasions

6A54—Well Fitting High Cut Shoe. Soft Black kid vamp. White "Wyclo" Guaranteed Cloth Laced Top. Recede toe. Louis heel. Sizes: 2½ to 7. Widths C, D and E. **$3.89**

6A320—Infant's Soft Soled Button Shoes of Black Patent Leather with Red, White or Light Blue kid tops. Sizes: 1 to 4. A price opportunity—three pairs for **$1.30** or per pair.................. **.45**

6A53—Extremely Smart High Cut Shoe. Havana Brown Pliable Kid Vamp. White "Wyclo" guaranteed cloth laced top. Recede toe. Louis heel. Sizes: 2½ to 7. Widths C, D and E. **$3.89**

6A34 The "Sylvan" Battleship Gray Soft Kid Leather Pump. Oxidized ornament on vamp and fancy strap. Smart recede toe. Concave heel. Sizes: 2½ to 8. Widths C, D and E. **$2.98**

6A57—Patent Leather "Lavalliere" Pump. Oxidized Buckle on strap. Tailored bow on vamp. Medium round toe. Concave heel. Sizes: 2½ to 8. Widths C, D and E.............. **$2.59**

6A26 The "Sylvan" Havana Brown Soft Kid Leather Pump. Oxidized ornament on vamp and fancy strap. Smart recede toe. Concave heel. Sizes: 2½ to 8. Widths C, D and E. **$2.98**

6A59—The "Classic." A high grade Patent Leather Pump. Non-slip lining. Trimmed with two white buttons. Slightly recede toe. Concave heel. Sizes: 2½ to 8. Widths C, D and E..................... **$2.59**

6A58—Gun Metal Leather 2 strap Pump. Medium round toe. Cuban heel. Sizes: 2½ to 8. Widths C, D and E.............. **$2.49**

Boy "Scout" Shoes

6A233—The "Scout" Shoe of Pliable Gray Ooze Leather. Durable Never-rip welt and chrome sole—no other sole gives better service. Sizes: 6 to 8, **$1.35**; 8½ to 11, **$1.49**; 11½ to 2, **$1.85**; 2½ to 5½, **$2.25**.

6A49—Black Velveteen 2 strap Pump. Good weight soles. Round toe. Medium heel. Sizes: 2½ to 8. Widths C, D and E.. **$1.49**

6A56—Instep Strap "Mary Jane" High Grade Patent Leather Pump. Wide toe. Low heel. Tailored bow. Sizes: 2½ to 8.. **$2.39**

6A232—The same style shoe as 6A233, but in Brown Ooze stock, same prices as above.

6A50—Gun Metal Leather "Mary Jane" Colonial Pump. Non-slip lining. Round toe. Low heel. Sizes: 2½ to 8. Widths C, D and E. **$2.39**

6A68—White Sea Island Canvas High Cut Button Boot. Milo steel riveted buttons. New recede toe. Canvas covered spool heel. White finished sole. *Sizes:* 2½ to 7. Widths C, D and E.
$2.69

Seasonable White Shoes
For
Sport, Walking, Street and Dress Wear

6A55—Well Arched White Canvas High Cut Laced Boot. Slightly recede toe. White finished Concave heel. and sole. *Sizes:* 2½ to 7. Widths C, D and E.
$2.29

6A67—Sport Oxford of White Sea Island Canvas. Guaranteed light tread white rubber sole. New recede toe. Canvas covered spool heel, leather top lift. *Sizes:* 2½ to 7. Widths C, D and E.... **$1.85**

6A64—Colonial Pump of Durable White Canvas. New recede toe. Concave Cuban heel. Good weight sole. White metal buckle. *Sizes:* 2½ to 8. Widths C, D and E..................... **$1.69**

6A65—White Canvas "Mary Jane" made on Perry Dame's Round Toe Last. White Rubber Soles and Low Rubber Heels. *Sizes:* 2½ to 8. Widths C, D and E....................... **$1.59**

6A61—Cross Strap Dress Pump of Serviceable Canvas. Tailored bow on vamp. New recede toe. Concave heel. *Sizes:* 2½ to 8. Widths C, D and E....................... **$1.69**

6A70—Smart White Canvas Two Strap Pump. Tailored bow on vamp. Medium round toe. White finished heel and sole. *Sizes:* 2½ to 8. Widths C, D and E........................ **$1.69**

6A71—Extra Strong Canvas Tennis Oxfords. Pliable corrugated rubber soles. Colors:—White or Black Canvas. *Sizes:* Children's 6 to 10½, **.59**; Misses' 11 to 2, **.69**; Ladies' 2½ to 7, **.69**; Boys' and Youths' 11 to 5½, **.69**.

6A69—"Kewpie" White Canvas Colonial Pump. Fancy pearl ornament on vamp. Recede toe. White finished heel and sole. *Sizes:* 2½ to 7. Widths C, D and E........................ **$1.69**

Three Exceptional Shoes For Sport Wear

6A62—The "Campus" Sport Oxford of Durable White Canvas. Guaranteed white rubber sole and low rubber heel. Round toe. *Sizes:* 2½ to 7. Widths C, D and E........... **$1.65**

6A60—The "Columbia" High Cut Sport Boot of Superior White Canvas. Guaranteed White Rubber Sole. Round toe. Low rubber heel. *Sizes:* 2½ to 7. Widths C, D and E. **$1.89**

6A66—The "University" White Canvas Sport Oxford. White Kid Ball Strap. Guaranteed White Fibre Sole. Round toe. White Rubber Heel. *Sizes:* 2½ to 7. Widths C, D and E **$1.98**

6A117—Black Patent Leather Dress Shoe. Fast Black Cloth buttoned top. Stylish plain toe. Spool heel. *Sizes:* 2½ to 8. Widths C, D and E **$2.75**
6A118—Same style may be had with Gun Metal Leather vamp **$2.75**

6A80—Black Gun Metal Leather Shoe. Gray Cloth Top. Plain toe. Concave heel, rubber top lift. *Sizes:* 2½ to 8. Widths C, D and E. **$2.75**
6A81—Same style with black cloth top .. **$2.75**

6A89—Gun Metal Leather Laced Boot. Gray cloth top. Concave Heel. *Sizes:* 2½ to 8. Widths C, D and E. **$2.75**
6A90—Same style with Black Cloth Top, same price.

6A78—Patent Leather Buttoned Shoe. Black Cloth Top. Round Toe. Cuban heel. *Sizes:* 2½ to 8. Widths C, D and E. **$2.39**

6A91—Carefully Made Black Velveteen Buttoned Shoe. Concave Cuban heel. Close trimmed dressed weight sole. Medium round toe. *Sizes:* 2½ to 8. Widths C, D and E **$2.15**

6A74—The Baby Doll. Patent Leather. Black Cloth Top. Wide toe. Low heel. *Sizes:* 2½ to 8. Widths C, D and E **$2.65**
6A75—Same style with Gun Metal Leather Vamp, same price.

6A76—The "Baby Doll" Patent Leather, Laced. Black Cloth Top. Wide toe. Low heel. *Sizes:* 2½ to 8. Widths C, D and E.... **$2.65**
6A77—Same style Gun Metal Leather Vamp.. **$2.65**

6A87—Buttoned Shoe of Chrome Tanned Patent Leather with Silk Brocade Quarter. Slightly recede toe. Spanish heel. *Sizes:* 2½ to 7. Widths C, D and E... **$2.50**

6A84—High Cut Laced Boot. Soft Black Kid Vamps and Tops. Perforated Black Patent Leather Quarter. Recede Toe. Concave Heel. *Sizes:* 2½ to 7. Widths C, D and E. **$3.89**

6A121—Black Patent Leather Dress Shoe with Soft Dull Black Kid Top. Concave Cuban Heel with Rubber Top Lift. *Sizes:* 2½ to 8. Widths C, D and E **$2.89**

6A92—High Laced Dress Shoe. Black Patent Leather Vamp with Black Cloth "Wave Top" Uppers. Smart Plain Toe. Concave Cuban Heel. *Sizes:* 2½ to 8. Widths C, D and E.... **$2.98**

6A82—High Cut Laced. Patent Leather Vamp. Dull Kid Quarter. Concave Heel, Rubber Lift. *Sizes:* 2½ to 8. C, D and E. **$3.15**
6A83—Same Style with Gun Metal Leather Vamp, same price.

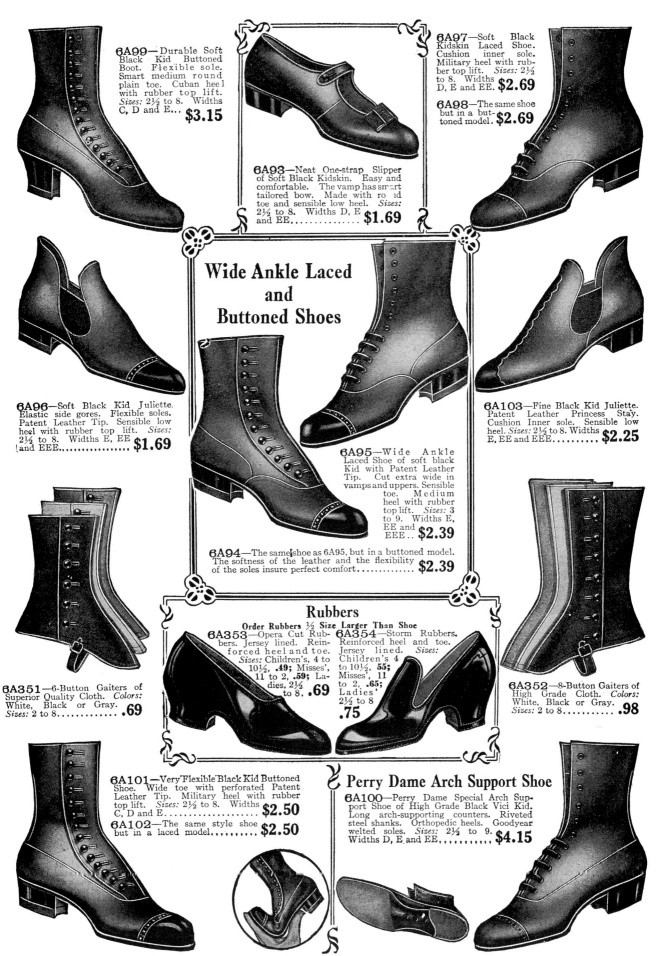

6A99—Durable Soft Black Kid Buttoned Boot. Flexible sole. Smart medium round plain toe. Cuban heel with rubber top lift. *Sizes:* 2½ to 8. Widths C, D and E... **$3.15**

6A93—Neat One-strap Slipper of Soft Black Kidskin. Easy and comfortable. The vamp has smart tailored bow. Made with round toe and sensible low heel. *Sizes:* 2½ to 8. Widths D, E and EE.............. **$1.69**

6A97—Soft Black Kidskin Laced Shoe. Cushion inner sole. Military heel with rubber top lift. *Sizes:* 2½ to 8. Widths D, E and EE. **$2.69**

6A98—The same shoe but in a buttoned model. **$2.69**

Wide Ankle Laced and Buttoned Shoes

6A96—Soft Black Kid Juliette. Elastic side gores. Flexible soles. Patent Leather Tip. Sensible low heel with rubber top lift. *Sizes:* 2½ to 8. Widths E, EE and EEE.................. **$1.69**

6A95—Wide Ankle Laced Shoe of soft black Kid with Patent Leather Tip. Cut extra wide in vamps and uppers. Sensible toe. Medium heel with rubber top lift. *Sizes:* 3 to 9. Widths E, EE and EEE.. **$2.39**

6A94—The same shoe as 6A95, but in a buttoned model. The softness of the leather and the flexibility of the soles insure perfect comfort............. **$2.39**

6A103—Fine Black Kid Juliette. Patent Leather Princess Stay. Cushion Inner sole. Sensible low heel. *Sizes:* 2½ to 8. Widths E, EE and EEE......... **$2.25**

Rubbers

Order Rubbers ½ Size Larger Than Shoe

6A353—Opera Cut Rubbers. Jersey lined. Reinforced heel and toe. *Sizes:* Children's, 4 to 10½, **.49**; Misses', 11 to 2, **.59**; Ladies, 2½ to 8. **.69**

6A354—Storm Rubbers. Reinforced heel and toe. Jersey lined. *Sizes:* Children's 4 to 10½, **.55**; Misses', 11 to 2, **.65**; Ladies' 2½ to 8 **.75**

6A351—6-Button Gaiters of Superior Quality Cloth. *Colors:* White, Black or Gray. *Sizes:* 2 to 8............. **.69**

6A352—8-Button Gaiters of High Grade Cloth. *Colors:* White, Black or Gray. *Sizes:* 2 to 8........... **.98**

6A101—Very Flexible Black Kid Buttoned Shoe. Wide toe with perforated Patent Leather Tip. Military heel with rubber top lift. *Sizes:* 2½ to 8. Widths C, D and E..................... **$2.50**

6A102—The same style shoe but in a laced model,........ **$2.50**

Perry Dame Arch Support Shoe

6A100—Perry Dame Special Arch Support Shoe of High Grade Black Vici Kid. Long arch-supporting counters. Riveted steel shanks. Orthopedic heels. Goodyear welted soles. *Sizes:* 2½ to 9. Widths D, E and EE,.......... **$4.15**

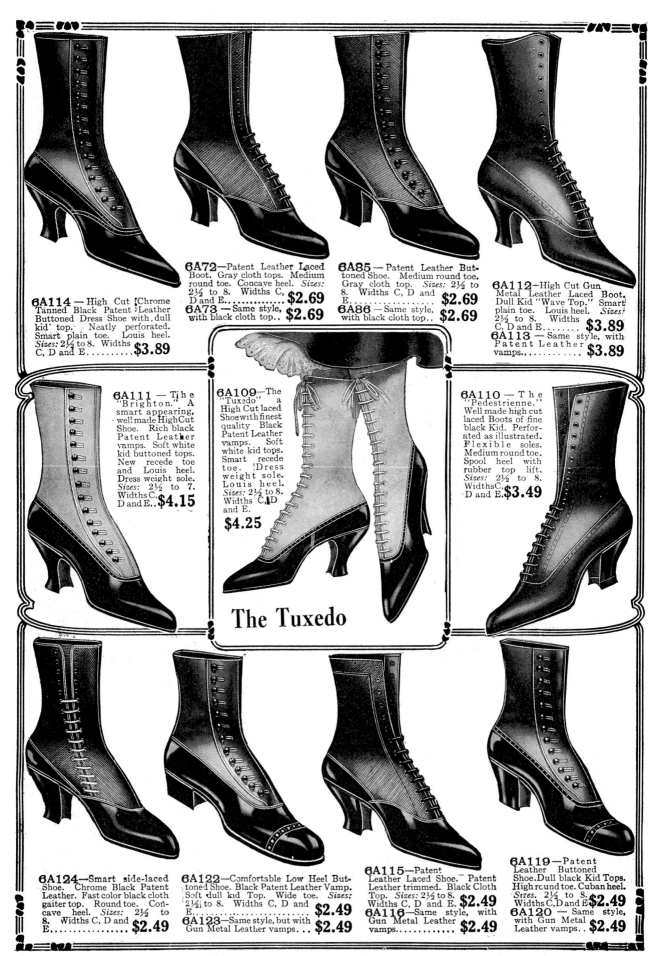

6A114 — High Cut Chrome Tanned Black Patent Leather Buttoned Dress Shoe with dull kid top. Neatly perforated. Smart plain toe. Louis heel. *Sizes:* 2½ to 8. Widths C, D and E.........**$3.89**

6A72 — Patent Leather Laced Boot. Gray cloth tops. Medium round toe. Concave heel. *Sizes:* 2½ to 8. Widths C, D and E.............**$2.69**
6A73 — Same style, with black cloth top..**$2.69**

6A85 — Patent Leather Buttoned Shoe. Medium round toe. Gray cloth top. *Sizes:* 2½ to 8. Widths C, D and E.............**$2.69**
6A86 — Same style, with black cloth top..**$2.69**

6A112 — High Cut Gun Metal Leather Laced Boot. Dull Kid "Wave Top." Smart plain toe. Louis heel. *Sizes:* 2½ to 8. Widths C, D and E.......**$3.89**
6A113 — Same style, with Patent Leather vamps.............**$3.89**

6A111 — The "Brighton." A smart appearing, well made High Cut Shoe. Rich black Patent Leather vamps. Soft white kid buttoned tops. New recede toe and Louis heel. Dress weight sole. *Sizes:* 2½ to 7. Widths C, D and E..**$4.15**

6A109 — The "Tuxedo" a High Cut laced Shoe with finest quality Black Patent Leather vamps. Soft white kid tops. Smart recede toe. Dress weight sole. Louis heel. *Sizes:* 2½ to 8. Widths C, D and E. **$4.25**

The Tuxedo

6A110 — The "Pedestrienne." Well made high cut laced Boots of fine black Kid. Perforated as illustrated. Flexible soles. Medium round toe. Spool heel with rubber top lift. *Sizes:* 2½ to 8. Widths C, D and E. **$3.49**

6A124 — Smart side-laced Shoe. Chrome Black Patent Leather. Fast color black cloth gaiter top. Round toe. Concave heel. *Sizes:* 2½ to 8. Widths C, D and E.................**$2.49**

6A122 — Comfortable Low Heel Buttoned Shoe. Black Patent Leather Vamp. Soft dull kid Top. Wide toe. *Sizes:* 2½ to 8. Widths C, D and E.............**$2.49**
6A123 — Same style, but with Gun Metal Leather vamps...**$2.49**

6A115 — Patent Leather Laced Shoe. Patent Leather trimmed. Black Cloth Top. *Sizes:* 2½ to 8. Widths C, D and E. **$2.49**
6A116 — Same style, with Gun Metal Leather vamps.............**$2.49**

6A119 — Patent Leather Buttoned Shoe. Dull black Kid Tops. High round toe. Cuban heel. *Sizes:* 2½ to 8. Widths C, D and E. **$2.49**
6A120 — Same style, with Gun Metal Leather vamps.. **$2.49**

6A220— Patent Leather Laced Shoe. Black Cloth top. Sizes: 7 to 8, **$1.50;** 8½ to 11, **$1.75;** 11½ to 2, **$2.25;** 2½ to 6, **$2.50.**
6A221—Same style with Gun Metal Leather Vamp, same prices.

Misses', Girls' and Children's Shoes

All Made on the Natural Foot Shape Perry Dame Last

6A209—Patent Leather "Mary Jane" Ankle Strap Pump. Silk bow on vamp. Sizes: 7 to 8, **$1.49;** 8½ to 11, **$1.75;** 11½ to 2, **$2.19;** 2½ to 6, **$2.45.**

6A210—Black Patent Leather 2 Strap Pump. Silk bow on vamp. Sizes: 7 to 8, **$1.49;** 8½ to 11, **$1.75;** 11½ to 2, **$2.19;** 2½ to 6, **$2.45.**

6A219—"Baby Doll" Buttoned Black Patent Leather Shoe with fast black cloth top. Sizes: 7 to 8, **$1.50;** 8½ to 11, **$1.75;** 11½ to 2, **$2.25;** 2½ to 6, **$2.50.**

6A213—High Cut Gun Metal Leather Buttoned Shoe. Soft black kid top. Sizes: 8½ to 11, **$1.98;** 11½ to 2, **$2.35;** 2½ to 7, **$2.60.**
6A212—Same style with Patent Leather Vamp, same prices.

6A208—White Canvas Two-Strap Pump with Tailored Bow. Sizes: 7 to 8, **$.98;** 8½ to 11, **$1.15;** 11½ to 2, **$1.35;** 2½ to 6, **$1.49.**

6A211—Ankle Strap "Mary Jane" White Canvas Pump with tailored bow. Sizes: 7 to 8, **$.98;** 8½ to 11, **$1.15;** 11½ to 2, **$1.49;** 2½ to 6, **$1.69.**

6A207—Gun Metal Leather "Mary Jane" Ankle Strap Colonial Pump. Sizes: 7 to 8, **$1.49;** 8½ to 11, **$1.75;** 11½ to 2, **$2.25;** 2½ to 6, **$2.50.**

6A218—Blucher Cut Laced Boot. Fine quality Gun Metal Leather vamps with dull kid tops. Sizes: 7 to 8, **$1.49;** 8½ to 11, **$1.65;** 11½ to 2, **$1.98;** 2½ to 6, **$2.29.**

6A226—Tan Kid Buttoned Shoe, with perforated tip. Sizes: 7 to 8, **$1.39;** 8½ to 11, **$1.59;** 11½ to 2, **$1.89;** 2½ to 6, **$2.35.**

The "Outwear All" Shoe for Boys

6A225—The "Outwear All" Laced Boot for Boys. Strong Black Gun Metal Leather. Blucher cut and made with copper tip to protect the toe against the wear occasioned by stubbing. Sizes: 8 to 13½, **$2.10.**

COPPER TOE GUARD

6A214—Black Patent Leather Buttoned Shoe with dull kid top. Sizes: 7 to 8, **$1.49;** 8½ to 11, **$1.75;** 11½ to 2, **$2.19;** 2½ to 6, **$2.39.**
6A215—The same style as 6A214, but with Gun Metal Leather Vamp, at the same prices.

6A223 Boys' Dress Shoe. Black Patent Leather Vamp with perforated tip. Dull Leather top. Sizes: 9 to 13½, **$2.15;** 1 to 6, **$2.50.**
6A222—The same style as 6A223, but Gun Metal Leather Vamp, at the same prices.

6A217—White Canvas Buttoned Shoes. Selected Leather Soles. Sizes: 7 to 8, **$1.05;** 8½ to 11, **$1.25;** 11½ to 2, **$1.55;** 2½ to 6, **$1.75.**

6A216—Black Vici Kid Buttoned Shoe with Perforated Patent Tip. Sizes: 7 to 8, **$1.39;** 8½ to 11, **$1.59;** 11½ to 2, **$1.89;** 2½ to 6, **$2.25.**

6A224—Boys' Blucher Shoe. Durable Black Gun Metal Leather vamps with dull leather tops. Sizes: 9 to 13½, **$2.15;** 1 to 6, **$2.50.**

Serviceable Shoes for Children and Infants

Flexible Turned Sole, Natural Foot Shape Shoes

6A307—High Cut Buttoned Shoe. Natural Foot Shape Last. Patent Leather Vamp. Soft dull kid top with Patent Leather Collar. *Sizes:* 4 to 8.......... **$1.69**

6A306—High Cut Buttoned Shoe. Fine Black Patent Leather Vamp. Soft white kid top with Patent Leather collar. *Sizes:* 4 to 8... **$1.75**

6A308—Black Patent Leather Buttoned Shoe. Soft Red Kid Top; with Patent Leather Collar. *Sizes:* 4 to 8... **$1.69**

6A301—"Mary Jane" Patent Leather Ankle Strap Pump. Tailored bow. *Sizes:* 2 to 5 without heel, .89; 5½ to 8, with heel, **$1.15.**

Children's Roman Sandal

6A305—Infant's Barefoot Sandal of White Chrome Leather or Tan Calfskin. Flexible leather sole. State Color. *Sizes:* 1 to 5. Two pairs, **$1.35.** One pair, .69.

6A303—"Mary Jane" Ankle Strap Pump of White Canvas with ribbon bow on vamp. *Sizes:* 2 to 5 without heel, .75; 5½ to 8 with heel, .89.

6A304 Five-strap Black Patent Leather Roman Sandal. Tailored bow on vamp. *Sizes:* 2 to 5 without heel, **$1.45;** 5½ to 8 with heel, **$1.59.**

6A302—2 Strap Black Patent Leather Pump with ribbon bow. *Sizes:* 2 to 5 without heel, .95; 5½ to 8 with heel **$1.15.**

6A316—Laced Shoe. Black Patent Leather vamp. Black Cloth Top. Flexible Turned Sole. *Sizes:* 2 to 5 without heel, **$1.19;** 5½ to 8 with heel, **$1.39.**

6A315—Golden Brown Vici Kid Buttoned Shoe. *Sizes:* 2 to 5 without heel, **$1.25;** 5½ to 8 with heel, **$1.45.**

6A311—Laced Shoe. Soft Black Kid with Patent Leather tip. *Sizes:* 2 to 5 without heel, .79; 5½ to 8 with heel, .98.

6A309—Black Kid Buttoned Shoe with Patent Leather Tip. *Sizes:* 2 to 5 without heel, .79; 5½ to 8 with heel, .98.

6A310—Dress Shoe of Patent Leather. Black Cloth Top. *Sizes:* 2 to 5 without heel, **$1.19;** 5½ to 8 with heel, **$1.35.**

6A312—Patent Leather Shoe with Black Velveteen Buttoned Top. *Sizes:* 2 to 5 without heel, **$1.19;** 5½ to 8 with heel, **$1.35.**

3A314—Black Patent Leather Buttoned Shoe with dull kid top. *Sizes:* 2 to 5 without heel, **$1.25;** 5½ to 8 with heel, **$1.45.**

6A313—Black Patent Leather Shoe with soft white kid top. *Sizes:* 2½ to 5 without heel, **$1.25;** 5½ to 8 with heel, **$1.45.**

Attractive Dresses for Juniors

1A702
$2<u>69</u>

1A703—White Galatea Middy Dress. Deep pointed Yoke. Two box plaits from yoke to pockets. Envelope Patch Pockets of Galatea and Linene to match collar and cuffs. Plain skirt. Invisible front closing. *Colors:* White trimmed with blue or all white. *Sizes:* 13, 15 and 17 years. **$1.69**

1A703
$1<u>69</u>

See Size
Scale on
Page 104

1A701
$2<u>25</u>

1A701—Carefully made Dress of Serviceable French Linon. White Piqué Hemstitched Collar and Cuffs. The Belt is embroidered in white, passes through Linon loops and so adjusts the fulness. Pointed patch pockets embroidered to match the belt. *Colors:* Copenhagen, tan or rose. *Sizes:* 13, 15 and 17 years......**$2.25**

1A702—Sport Smock Dress of Linene and Galatea. Below the front yoke, hand smocking accomplishes the gathers. Linene and White Galatea Collar. Black Repp tie. Front closing and Turned-back cuffs piped with white Galatea. Plain White Galatea Skirt. Invisible Front Closing. *Colors:* Copenhagen, rose or apple-green smock. Plain white skirt. *Sizes:* 13, 15 and 17 years......**$2.69**

1A705—Dress of Flowered Voile, trimmed with silk piping and bows. Hemstitched White Organdie Collar, with Val edge. Sleeves have cuffs and lace edged ruffle. Silk Poplin Girdle. The tucked skirt is made with a yoke set off by a tucked ruffle. *Colors:* Pink, Copenhagen or lavender. *Sizes:* 13, 15, 17 years. **$3.98**

1A704
$5<u>98</u>

1A705
$3<u>98</u>

1A704—Frock of Fine White Net handsomely embroidered. Square neck finished with lace edge and silk rosette. Soft silk girdle. Sleeves of plain net have two silk edged ruffles. Four similar ruffles trim the skirt. *Colors:* White with pink or white with blue girdle, or all white. *Sizes:* 13, 15 and 17....**$5.98**

Junior Dresses for Sport, Everyday or Dress Wear

1A709— Sailor Dress of White Galatea. Simulated double closing. French Linon Collar, braid trimmed, embroidered with star to match sleeve design. Braid trimmed Linon cuffs. Panel front skirt. Wide Galatea band across back, laced to pockets in front. *Colors:* White with blue or all white. *Sizes:* 13, 15 and 17 years.. **$1.98**

1A708—White Embroidered Voile Dress, trimmed with Val lace. Val panel on waist front outlined with embroidered Voile. Back of waist is tucked on either side of invisible closing. Three-section skirt of tucked and embroidered voile. Silk belt with smart bow. *Colors:* White with blue or white with pink belt or all white. *Sizes:* 13, 15 and 17 years **$2.98**

1A706—Beautiful Dress of All Over Embroidered Organdie. Made alike both front and back. Center panel on waist of pin tucked Organdie and lace. Organdie ruffles on sleeves with lace insertion. Two-section skirt of All Over Embroidered Organdie, plain White Organdie applied hem. *Colors:* White with maize or blue girdle, or all white. *Sizes:* 13, 15 and 17........ **$4.98**

1A709
$1.98

1A710
$2.98

1A710—Dress of Striped Voile with an all-over floral effect. Plain white Voile collar with hemstitching and picot edged plaiting which also trims the white voile cuffs and patch pockets. Slightly gathered skirt joined to waist by the belt. Convenient front closing with pearl button trimming. *Colors:* Blue, pink or lavender. *Sizes,* 13, 15 and 17 years.. **$2.98**

1A706
$4.98

1A708
$2.98

Size Scale for Junior Dresses

Yrs.	Bust	
13	33 in.	31 in.
15	35 in.	32 in.
17	37 in.	34 in.

1A707
$1.98

1A707—Tailored Sport Dress of Striped Linene. Plain Linene to match, piped with white, supplies the collar and cuffs. Combined with the material it makes the smart patch pockets on skirt. Trim belt of plain Linene. *Colors:* Tan and blue, tan and green, or tan and rose. *Sizes:* 13, 15 and 17 years.. **$1.98**

Junior Coats and a Suit

3A301—Well made Coat of Velour Check. Deep square collar. In front the belt fastens to the patch pockets with plain steel buttons. Similar buttons trim the cuffs and effect the closing. Colors: Black and White or Brown and White Velour Cotton Check. Sizes: 13, 15 and 17 years. Back Length 32 inches.....**$3.29**

3A304—Modish Coat of White Chinchilla. The deep square collar may be worn open at the throat, or closed, as pictured. The sectional belt crosses in front and fastens to the patch pockets with large white buttons. Sizes: 13, 15 and 17 years. Back Length 32 inches. White only..........**$4.98**

3A302—Smartly Tailored Coat of Good Quality Serge. The belt at waist distributes the fulness. The deep round collar and patch pockets are piped with green and trimmed with green centered buttons. Colors: blue or black, piped with green. Sizes: 13, 15 and 17 years. Back Length 32 ins...**$4.98**

Size Scale for Junior Suits and Coats

Years	Bust	Skirt
13	33 in.	33 in.
15	35 in.	35 in.
17	37 in.	37 in.

3A304
$4.98

3A302
$4.98

3A301
$3.29

4A201
$10.98

3A303
$5.98

4A201—Smartly tailored Suit of Fine Quality All Wool Serge. Well fitting coat trimmed with buttons and silk in a contrasting shade. Fancy Sateen lining throughout. Smooth fitting skirt with overlapping front seam. Colors: Navy with green, Copenhagen with red or green with mustard. Sizes: 13, 15 and 17 years.......**$10.98**

3A303—New Model Coat of Black and White Wool Mixture with gold over plaid. The deep collar has notched revers and is trimmed with gold colored broadcloth and large novelty buttons. The patch pockets have Broadcloth tabs. Belted waist. Sizes: 13, 15 and 17 years.. Back Length about 37 inches........**$5.98**

Junior Coats and a Suit

3A305—New Style Black and White Striped Flannel Coat. Green broadcloth trims the collar, cuffs and patch pockets. The belt fastens to the patch pockets with novelty buttons. *Sizes:* 13, 15 and 17 years. Back Length about 32 inches...... **$4.98**

3A305
$4.98

3A308—Handsome Corduroy Coat. Deep Collar has notched revers and is trimmed with White Corduroy. Cuffs and patch pockets similarly trimmed. Novelty buttons. *Colors:* Coral, or Copenhagen with white, or white trimmed with coral. *Sizes:* 13, 15 and 17 years. Back Length about 32 inches........... **$5.98**

3A307—All Wool Serge Coat. Gracefully Cut Collar with striped silk overlay. Belt fastens to the slashed pockets in front. Button trimmed pointed turn-back cuffs, of the material. *Colors:* Copenhagen, navy, mustard or black. *Sizes:* 13, 15 and 17 years. Back Length about 36 inches. **$6.98**

3A308
$5.98

See Size
Scale on
Page 105

4A202
$7.98

3A306
$5.98

3A307
$6.98

3A306—Smartly Designed Coat of Black and White Shepherd Check, with a green over-plaid. Green Velour Cheviot trims the patch pockets, cuffs and deep square collar. A double row of white stitching further trims the collar, cuffs and pockets. Button trimmed belt at waist. *Sizes:* 13, 15 and 17 years. Back Length about 37 inches. **$5.98**

4A202—Suit of Black and White Check. Dresden Sateen lining. Square Collar has notched revers and Green Silk overlay. Buttons trim the belt, cuffs and pockets. Slight gathers at back of plain skirt beneath yoke. Patch pockets. *Sizes:* 13, 15 and 17 years.... **$7.98**

18A7—Becoming one-piece Dress for little girls made of serviceable Repp, attractively embroidered. It is designed with two strap pockets and a belt. It slips on over the head, and fastens at the neck with a lacing. *Colors:* White, pink or blue............ **.69**

18A2—Here is a pretty Dress of serviceable White Lawn Embroidery combined with plain pin-tucked lawn. The sleeves and the back of the neck are edged with lace. Silk ribbon bow on the belt in either Pink or Light Blue, as preferred. Back closing.....**.79**

18A1—A little girl's Empire Dress. It is made of fine quality Plaid Gingham combined with finest White Mercerized Repp. The waist is stylishly smocked in front, and the little coatee is detachable. Back closing. *Colors:* Blue combination plaid, or brown combination plaid; each combined with white............ **$1.25**

18A7
69¢

18A9
98¢

Charming Dresses
FOR
Little Girls

SIZES 2 to 6 YEARS

18A9—Dainty one-piece Dress of fine quality Chambray. Richly trimmed with Hand Smocking, white piping. It has an Empire belt. Slips on over the head and closes with pearl buttons and loops in front, as pictured. *Colors:* Cadet blue, rose-pink, or Nile green............. **.98**

18A6—"Party" Dress of exquisitely embroidered sheer White Organdie. It is trimmed with lace, a ribbon flower, and a silk ribbon belt. The back of the waist and the sleeves are of plain pin-tucked organdie. Back closing. Ribbon in Pink or Light Blue, as preferred.......... **$1.25**

18A8—Little girl's one-piece Middy Dress, made of strong White Linene and Plaid Gingham. It has a jaunty pocket, and fastens at the neck with a lacing, as pictured. *Colors:* White, with blue combination plaid; or white, with pink combination plaid....... **.59**

18A6
$1.25

18A2
79¢

18A1
$1.25

18A8
59¢

18A5
$1.49

18A5—The "Pretty Betty" model—an attractive little Empire Dress of fine quality Striped Burette Crêpe, a new material similar to Chambray. It is trimmed with fine White Piqué, fancy edging and pearl buttons. Full-length front closing. *Colors:* pink and white; or Copenhagen blue and white. **$1.49**

18A4—One-piece "Peter Pan" Dress for little girls. It is made of fine quality Chambray and Striped Gingham. The collar is trimmed with embroidery, and the Empire-belted waist is set off with pearl buttons. Front closing. *Colors:* Copenhagen blue and white combination; or pink and white combination.... **.98**

18A3—Very rich and delightfully becoming Empire Frock for dressy wear. It is made of fine White Organdie, handsomely trimmed with sheer embroidered organdie, Val lace and satin ribbon, in the newest style. Back closing. Pink or Light Blue ribbon, as preferred...... **$1.98**

18A4
98¢

18A3
$1.98

YOU MUST BE PLEASED OR YOUR MONEY BACK

22A8—One-piece Rompers of Fine Quality Chambray. Neat hemstitching on the White Linene collar and cuffs. Drop seat. Colors: Blue or tan, each trimmed with white. Sizes: 2 to 6 years .... .69

22A2 $1 69

Boys' Suits

22A2—Three-piece Sailor Suit of Durable White Galatea. Two pairs of pants are provided—one long and one short pair; both with slashed pockets. Red band on left sleeve. Detachable shield with blue star. Tie and Collar of blue Galatea. Sizes: 3 to 10 years. Ideal for beach wear. **$1.69**

22A4—Smartly Tailored Suit of Fine Quality Repp. Coat has simulated breast pocket and plaits at each side of front. New style patch pockets with loops through which the belt is drawn. Straight cut pants with slashed pockets. Colors: Tan or blue trimmed with white; also all white. Sizes: 3 to 8 years **$1.39**

22A5—Cool, Attractive Suit of Fine Quality Striped Percale. Belted coat with button trimmed plaits. White Linene collar, cuffs, belt and binding. Tassel cord tie. Straight cut pants. Colors: Navy blue and white or brown and white. Sizes: 3 to 8 years .... .79

Fast color materials, which may be laundered without hesitancy.

22A8 69¢

22A4 $1 39

22A5 79¢

22A3—Another Jaunty Suit to be worn with or without a blouse. Awning Striped Linon Coat, belted at the waist. Straight cut pants with side pockets. Coat Colors: White ground with tan or blue stripes; pants, all white. Sizes: 3 to 8 years. **$1.29**

22A6—Serviceable Linon Wash Suit. Belted coat with patch pockets, box plaits and round collar. Tassel cord tie at neck. Straight cut pants. Colors: Tan trimmed with blue, or blue trimmed with white. Sizes: 3 to 8 years .... .98

22A9—Child's Two-piece Dutch Suit of Serviceable Linene. The waist and pants are joined together with large pearl buttons. Colors: Blue striped waist with blue pants, or tan striped waist with blue pants. Sizes: 2 to 6 years ... .55

22A7—Handsome New Style Norfolk Suit of High-grade Galatea. Coat has two box plaits in front and one in back. Smart breast pocket and detachable shield. Straight cut pants with side pockets. Colors: White trimmed with fast color blue linene; also all white. Sizes: 3 to 10 years **$1.19**

22A9 55¢

22A1 $1 49

22A1—Perfect-fitting Coat Suit of Superior Quality Beach Cloth for wear with or without a blouse. The belted coat is made with pockets. The straight cut pants have side pockets. The smooth fitting collar has notched revers. Colors: Tan with Navy stripes, or solid tan. Sizes: 3 to 10 years. A serviceable, easily laundered suit **$1.49**

22A3 $1 29

22A6 98¢

22A7 $1 19

Boys' Suits

22A10—Well Tailored Pinch-back Coat Suit of high-grade Repp. The coat is made with a front yoke, and plaits. Stitched belt at waist. Silk-finished White Whipcord Collar, with red repp tie. Straight cut pants with pockets. *Colors:* Tan, blue or white, trimmed as above. *Sizes:* 3 to 8 years. A manly little model for dress wear..........**$1.98**

22A12—Boy's Suit of Good Grade Linene. The belt has patch pockets trimmed with White Linene. Tassel cord tie at neck. Straight cut pants, provided with side pockets. *Colors:* Tan or blue, each trimmed with White Linene collar and cuffs and a neat Vestee of White Linene. *Sizes:* 3 to 8 years. A cool, comfortable summer suit..........**.98**

22A13—This Ideal Four-Piece Outfit is of French Linon, combined with Chambray. It consists of a Belted White Linon Coat with colored Chambray trimming, a pair of White French Linon straight-cut Pants, a pair of colored Chambray straight-cut pants, and a colored Chambray Peak Cap. *Colors:* White and blue or White and Tan combination. *Sizes:* 3 to 8 years... **$1.19**

22A18—Cool, One-piece, Striped Linen Rompers. Trimmed as illustrated with plain linon to match. Drop Seat. *Colors:* Blue and white, or tan and white. *Sizes:* 2 to 6 years.. ....**.69**

22A13 **$1.19**

22A12 **98¢**

22A18 **69¢**

22A10 **$1.98**

22A14—French-finished Linen Suit. In front, the coat is plaited from yoke to belt. Collar, cuffs, tie and belt of White Repp. Two novel patch pockets. Straight cut pants with slashed pockets. *Colors:* Cadet blue or tan. *Sizes:* 3 to 8 years. **$1.19**

22A17—Two-piece "Oliver Twist" Suit of Easily Laundered Repp. It is trimmed with colored Linene and has lacing at the neck. Waist and pants fasten with buttonholes and pearl buttons. *Colors:* White suit trimmed in blue or tan. *Sizes:* 3 to 7 years.......... **.59**

22A15—Middy Suit of Durable Linene. The Middy has a square back, collar and cuffs trimmed with straps. Slip-knot tie at neck. Straight-cut pants. Readily laundered. *Colors:* Tan suit trimmed with blue; or all tan. *Sizes:* 3 to 8 years...... **.79**

22A16—Boys' Wash Suit of Serviceable White Linene with striped trimming. Tassel cord tie at neck. Straight cut pants. *Colors:* White with blue, or white with pink. *Sizes:* 3 to 8 years. Will wash splendidly.......... **.65**

22A14 **$1.19**

22A15 **79¢**

22A11 **$1.49**

22A17 **59¢**

22A11—Splendid Norfolk Coat Suit for boys from 3 to 10 years. Made of fine quality Striped Galatea, trimmed with solid White Galatea embroidered with floss to match. Black repp tie. Straight cut pants with side pockets. *Colors:* Navy blue and white or brown and white. A well made, durable suit.......... **$1.49**

22A16 **65¢**

Girls' and Children's Coats

20A53—Attractive Coat of fine quality Serge. Extremely good for general wear. Sateen lining throughout. The collar, cuffs and belt, and the button centers are of Copenhagen Pongee. Collar is supplemented by an overlay of embroidered Organdie. The coat's fulness is adjusted by means of the belt. *Colors:* Navy blue trimmed with Copenhagen, or Copenhagen trimmed with navy. *Sizes:* 6 to 14 years........................... **$4.98**

20A1—Little Girl's Serviceable Coat of good quality woven Shepherd Check. Lined throughout with Sateen. Cadet blue trimming on the revers, cuffs, and belt which is also finished with a buckle. *Colors:* Black and white check with cadet blue trimming. *Sizes:* 2 to 6 years. **$2.19**

20A51—Girl's Utility Coat of Cotton Plaid with "Wolnap" finish. The deep, square collar is trimmed with Green Repp and metal buttons. Cuffs and patch pockets trimmed to match. Note the new "throw-tie" belt. *Colors:* Black and white with green trimming. *Sizes:* 6 to 14 years......... **$2.98**

20A1
$2.19

20A53
$4.98

20A52
$3.98

20A51
$2.98

20A54
$4.49

20A2
$4.98

20A52—Smart Coat of Excellent quality woven Check. Carefully tailored. Full Sateen lined. Belt and pockets cut in novel outline. Small round collar with notched revers and an overlay of embroidered Organdie, forming a deep point in back. Oxidized silver buttons form the closing and trim the cuffs and pockets. *Colors:* Black and white check. *Sizes:* 6 to 14 years. **$3.98**

20A2—Fashionable Dress Coat of All Wool Serge for Little Girls. Full plaited skirt all around. Silk girdle finished with a dainty rosette. Lined throughout with Sateen. White hemstitched piqué collar and cuffs. *Colors:* Navy blue or Copenhagen, each trimmed with a Copenhagen girdle. *Sizes:* 2 to 6 years. Exceptional Value... **$4.98**

20A54—Smartly Tailored Coat of Gray Green and Black Mixture. Pretty Green Broadcloth trims the collar, cuffs and patch pockets. Coat may be worn buttoned to the throat or with the revers turned back. *Sizes:* 6 to 14 years............... **$4.49**

Girls' Stylish and Inexpensive Dresses

18A51—A practical two-piece Middy Dress of fine quality White Linene with fast-color Linene trimming. The Middy is made with lacings at both sides of the bottom and at the neck. The skirt is full side-plaited and is joined to a sleeveless underwaist which buttons in back. *Colors:* White trimmed with rose-pink or with blue, as preferred. *Sizes:* 6 to 14 years............................**.98**

18A52—Stylish Plaid Gingham Wash Dress. It is made with a prettily embroidered panel of solid color gingham in the front of the waist, and solid color gingham cuffs. The collar is of white piqué, finished at the neck with a smart black velvet bow. Full side-plaited skirt with fashionable fold at the bottom. Solid color gingham belt. Closes in back. *Colors:* Rose pink or blue combination. *Sizes:* 6 to 14 years.... **.79**

18A53—A Dainty Dress of excellent quality Embroidery in an attractive solid and eyelet pattern. The waist is made in the fashionable surplice style. The graceful double flounce skirt makes this dress an exceptionally becoming model. The back of the waist is made of pin-tucked lawn. A belt and rosette of Silk ribbon add just the right touch of color. Closes in back. *Colors:* White Dress with ribbon in pink or blue, as preferred. *Sizes:* 6 to 14 years................... **$1.25**

18A54—This pretty Dress of excellent quality Plaid Gingham is a new version of the popular Norfolk style. The embroidered collar, cuffs and pockets, and the belt, are made of fancy White Gabardine. Stylish box-plaited skirt. Closes in front with pearl buttons. *Colors:* Blue combination plaid, or tan combination plaid. *Sizes:* 6 to 14 years............ .... **$1.69**

18A51
98¢

18A55
$1.00

18A52
79¢

18A55—This Simple Little Dress is made of attractive Lawn Embroidery Flouncing. The plaited skirt and the front of the waist are made entirely of the embroidery. The back of the waist and the lace-edged sleeves are of fine pin-tucked lawn. Pin-tucked belt. Closes in back. White only. *Sizes:* 6 to 14 years........ **$1.00**

18A56—A Stylish New Model is this Dress of fine quality Plisse Crêpe in an attractive broad-striped pattern. The waist is made with a fashionable collar of self-material, neatly hemstitched. (Note small back view.) At the neck, a black velvet band trimmed with two pearl buckles lends a smart touch. The skirt is designed with two box pleats in front and an inverted plait in back; has two button-trimmed patch pockets and an attractive belt with black velvet straps across the front. Front closing. *Colors:* Blue or pink stripes on a white background, as preferred. *Sizes:* 6 to 14 years................. **$1.79**

18A54
$1.69

18A53
$1.25

18A56
$1.79

Girls' Dainty Dresses

18A57—Stylish Dress of fine quality Linene. It has an attractive surplice collar, turn-back cuffs and novel pocket trimming of White Fancy Gabardine, finished off with embroidered scallops. Belt of self-material. Closes in front. *Colors:* Pink, tan or cadet blue, each trimmed with white. *Sizes:* 6 to 14 years............ **$1.29**

18A58—A simple but attractive Empire Frock made of fine quality Flowered Plisse Crêpe. The collar and cuffs are made of cool-looking White Lawn edged with lace. The skirt is shirred entirely around and made with a dainty heading. Two attractive pouch pockets. Closes in front with beautiful pearl buttons. *Colors:* White background, with flowers in blue or pink, as preferred. *Sizes:* 6 to 14 years.. **$1.49**

18A59—Extremely dainty is this Dress of Embroidered Organdie and Voile. The fashionable Bolero style is a charming feature. Lace-trimmed embroidered organdie sections fall loosely over the waist in front, as pictured. The dainty double-flounced skirt is made of sheer Embroidered Organdie to match. An embroidery panel, outlined with lace, trims the front of the waist. Lace at the armholes, neck and sleeves. Sleeves are of pin-tucked lawn. Lustrous silk ribbon belt with bow. Back closing. *Colors:* White dress, with ribbon in blue, pink or white, as preferred. *Sizes:* 6 to 14 years........... **$1.98**

Descriptions of Dresses Shown On Facing Page

18A60—Here is a pretty new style Frock designed on Empire lines. It is a one-piece dress made of high grade Floral Voile combined with sheer White Organdie. The "Jumper" sections which fall loosely over the front and back of the White Organdie waist are richly trimmed with lace. Dainty Floral Voile frills at the neck and sleeves. The skirt is gracefully gathered around the waist-line and trimmed with two ruffles of self material. Closes in back with small pearl buttons. *Colors:* Floral Voile in a handsome rose color combination or green combination, each combined with White Organdie, as pictured. *Sizes:* 6 to 14 years. A beautiful frock for dressy wear... **$3.29**

18A61—This is a serviceable Wash Dress of good quality Chambray and Plaid Gingham combined. The front of the waist is made with two box plaits richly embroidered in Japanese style. The skirt is plaited all around. Belt is of the chambray and gingham prettily combined. Closes in front. *Colors:* Cadet blue, pink or tan, each with combination plaid to harmonize. *Sizes:* 6 to 14 years...... **$1.25**

18A62—The "Sport Girl's" Dress. It is a jaunty two-piece model made of fine quality White Galatea, combined with Blazer-striped Galatea. The slipover middy is smartly plaited at each side front and back. The belt fastens with pearl buttons at the left side. Silk lacing at the neck, drawn through reinforced eyelets. The skirt is full side-plaited, and is joined to a sleeveless muslin underwaist which closes in back. *Colors:* Green stripes, blue stripes or rose stripes, each combined with white. *Sizes:* 6 to 14 years..... **$1.98**

18A63—A Stylish Dress of High Grade Linon, with dainty lace-edged collar and cuffs of fine White Repp. The front of the waist is adorned with hand-smocking and two box plaits trimmed with beautiful pearl buttons. Box-plaited skirt with two hand-smocked pouch pockets. Attractive belt. Front closing. *Colors:* Tan, rose or cadet blue. *Sizes:* 6 to 14 years............ **$1.98**

18A64—Embroidered Organdie is an appropriate material for a Dressy Frock. In this beautiful Empire model the material is both sheer and dainty. The attractiveness of the front of the dress is also carried out in the back. It is beautifully trimmed with fine Val laces and tiny pin tucks, as pictured. Dainty bretelles over the shoulders. Exquisite satin ribbon belt, finished with two rosettes in front and a bow in back. Back closing. *Colors:* White dress, with ribbon in pink, blue or white, as preferred. *Sizes:* 6 to 14 years.... **$2.39**

18A65—This dainty two-piece Empire Dress is a handsome model. It is made of fine quality Linen, with a separate lace-trimmed guimpe of fine White Novelty Voile. Note the handsome silk embroidery on the front of the waist and on the fashionable pockets. The skirt is attractively gathered and plaited. Closes with fancy crocheted buttons. *Colors:* Copenhagen blue, pink or white. *Sizes:* 6 to 14 years. This dress is one of the very newest styles. **$2.69**

18A66—A Stylish Dress made of excellent quality Striped Gingham. The neat "Quaker" collar and cuffs are of White Piqué. At the neck is a novelty black velvet bow. Plaited skirt. An attractive feature is shown in the "shield" shape pockets which form loops for the belt to be drawn through. The belt is trimmed with a pearl buckle and pearl buttons. Closes in front. *Colors:* Rose-pink combination stripes, blue combination stripes, or green combination stripes. *Sizes:* 6 to 14 years......................... **$1.25**

18A57
$1.29

18A58
$1.49

18A59
$1.98

18A66
$1.25

18A63
$1.98

18A62
$1.98

18A64
$2.39

18A65
$2.69

18A60
$3.29

18A61
$1.25

FOR DESCRIPTIONS OF THESE DRESSES SEE FACING PAGE

Serviceable Dresses for Girls

18A70—This quaint Empire Frock is made of good quality Striped Gingham, with the waist part of solid color gingham. An attractive metal buckle trims the belt. The waist is cut on smart straight lines and the skirt is arranged in soft full plaits entirely around. Closes in front with beautiful pearl buttons and buttonholes. *Colors:* Pink and white, blue and white or tan and white. *Sizes:* 6 to 14 years. The beautiful Empire Style is very much in vogue this season for girls' dresses............................. **$1.00**

18A71—A Handsome Lace Dress. It is a beautiful model, dainty and rich in every way. An ideal frock for graduation, confirmation or party wear. The soft white Shadow Lace is prettily arranged over a White Net foundation. Around the neck the lace is softly shirred in quaint "Bertha" fashion, with silk ribbon lending a dainty touch. The ruffle on the net underskirt is trimmed with two bands of silk ribbon and the sleeves are finished with ribbon-trimmed frills to match. Wide silk ribbon belt with bow. Closes in back. *Colors:* White dress with ribbon in pink, blue or white, as preferred.. **$3.98**

18A72—This splendid One-piece Dress is designed in an attractive new style. It is made of fine quality Chambray and Plaid Gingham. The peplum over the plaited skirt is ornamented with two braid-trimmed patch pockets. This dress is made to slip on over the head, and it fastens at the neck with a silk cord lacing, drawn through reinforced eyelets. *Colors:* Cadet blue, pink or tan, each trimmed with combination plaid to harmonize. *Sizes:* 6 to 14 years......................... **$1.19**

18A67—A wonderfully attractive Dress of fine quality Chambray and Plaid Gingham combined. The smart straight lines, the chic "Empire" effect and the graceful fulness of the plaited skirt make a most stylish model. The button-trimmed pockets are in the new flap style. Handsome silk cord tie at the neck. Buttons in front. *Colors:* Cadet blue or pink; each with plaid to match. *Sizes:* 6 to 14 years........................ **$2.19**

18A71 $3.98

18A72 $1.19

18A70 $1.00

18A68—A Dress of Pleasing Style, made of fine quality Repp with a guimpe effect. The embroidered "Jumper" sections fall loosely over the front of the waist and the skirt is stylishly plaited all around. Detachable belt with two scalloped flaps in pocket effect. Closes in front with small pearl buttons and buttonholes. *Colors:* Cadet blue, pink or all white. *Sizes:* 6 to 14 years.. **$1.49**

18A69 $2.25

18A69—A handsome two-piece Dress made of high grade, firmly woven Fancy Crash. The bottom of the coat is cut in smart scalloped outline. Collar, cuffs and detachable belt of the plain crash. The skirt is stylishly box-plaited all around and attached to a sleeveless underwaist of white muslin. Shield of plain crash stitched on the underwaist. Closes with beautiful pearl buttons *Colors:* Copenhagen blue or tan, each with contrasting striped coat. *Sizes:* 6 to 14 years................... **$2.25**

18A67 $2.19

18A68 $1.49

LOUNGING ROBES WITH CHARM & EASE

8A155
59c
CAP

14A3
$1.79
FLORAL CRÊPE

14A5
$2.49
SERPENTINE CRÊPE

14A1
$1.98
HAND EMB. JAPANESE CRÊPE

14A2
$1.29
CRÊPE

CRÊPE DE CHINE
14A4
$3.69

All These Robes Are Cut FULL WIDTH

14A1—Attractive imported Japanese Robe of excellent quality Japanese Crêpe. This robe is elaborately embroidered *by hand* in a heavy raised design. (Note small back view.) The sleeves are wide, and there is a sash-belt of self-material at the waist-line. *Colors:* rose-pink, Copenhagen blue or lavender. *Sizes:* 32 to 44 bust. You will find in this robe the comfort you desire. It washes beautifully.......... **$1.98**

14A2—A dainty House Robe of fine quality Crêpe, richly embroidered *by hand* with heavy silk floss. It is finished with white lawn collar and cuffs edged with lace. The skirt part is prettily gathered on an elastic cord at the waist-line. The pocket is also made with an elastic cord. *Colors:* lavender, Copenhagen blue, or a becoming shade of pink. *Sizes:* 32 to 46 bust................. **$1.29**

14A3—Beautiful Floral Crêpe Lounging Robe made in a lovely new style. The deep circular collar and graceful "butterfly wing" sleeves are trimmed with frills of lustrous self-color sateen. Sateen bow at the neck. *Colors:* navy blue background, with Copenhagen blue flowers; Copenhagen blue background, with tan flowers, or a beautiful lavender combination. *Sizes:* 32 to 46 bust.............. **$1.79**

14A4—An exquisitely rich and beautiful Robe for leisure hours. It is made of fine quality lustrous Crêpe de Chine. It is trimmed with dainty frills and little bows of fine satin ribbon, as pictured. The graceful lines of this robe lend themselves to any figure. *Colors:* rose color, Copenhagen blue or heliotrope; each trimmed with satin ribbon to match. *Sizes:* 32 to 46 bust................. **$3.69**

14A5—Fashionable one-piece Negligée of fine quality soft Serpentine Crêpe. It is designed in the latest "Tea-Jacket" model, exquisitely embroidered *by hand* with heavy silk floss. Accordion-plaited skirt part gathered on elastic cord. Satin Ribbon bow at the neck. White lawn sleeveless jacket lining. *Colors:* Copenhagen blue, rose-pink or heliotrope. *Sizes:* 32 to 46 bust... **$2.49**

8A155—Boudoir Cap in the new "Dutch Hood" effect. Made of fine White Net and Lace, trimmed with satin ribbon in *Pink* or *Light Blue,* as preferred...... **.59**

OUR GUARANTEE IS ABSOLUTE—SATISFACTION ASSURED

115

Dresses for the Porch or Morning Wear

14A51—Splendid quality Checked Gingham and solid color Linene make this pleasing morning dress. The lace edged collar and cuffs and the vestee are of sheer white hemstitched organdie. Front closing with pearl buttons. *Colors:* Blue and white, or pink and white. *Sizes:* 32 to 46 bust; skirt length 40 inches....... **$1.79**

14A53—A Practical Porch Dress of rich quality Linene. A new one-piece style, with an Empire yoke both back and front. The white Linene collar is richly embroidered and finished with a slipknot tie. The fulness of this somewhat loose fitting model is adjusted to the wearer's own liking by aid of the black patent leather belt drawn through loops at the waist-line. Closes in front with handsome pearl buttons. *Colors:* Blue or pink, with white collar embroidered to match and also all white, with white collar embroidered in blue. *Sizes:* 32 to 46 bust; skirt length 40 inches.................. **$2.39**

14A53
$2.39
LINENE

14A54—A very stylish Awning Striped Gingham of excellent quality is used in this Dress. The smart collar and cuffs of solid color chambray are trimmed with embroidered lawn, as illustrated. The smooth-fitting skirt is finished with two patch pockets made with inverted, button trimmed points of plain chambray. *Colors:* green combination, blue combination, tan combination or pink combination. *Sizes:* 32 to 46 bust; skirt length 40 inches. A serviceable dress for garden or porch wear. One that will launder well and keep its color... **$2.29**

14A51
$1.79
GINGHAM

14A52—This wonderfully attractive dress is a brand new style. It is made of superior quality Novelty Voile, combined with plain white Voile. The deep square-back collar and the cuffs are finished with a lace edge. A small silk ribbon bow trims the neck. The skirt is gracefully gathered. Long, graceful lines are achieved through the panels of contrasting voile on the side gores. The well crocheted sash-belt, with its long tassel ends, make this one of the smartest morning dresses of the season. Front fastening. *Colors:* White with blue, or white with lavender. *Sizes:* 32 to 46 bust; skirt length 40 inches... **$2.69**

14A52
$2.69
NOVELTY VOILE

14A54
$2.29
AWNING STRIPE GINGHAM

Morning Dresses for the House or Garden

14A57—Wash Dress of fine quality Checked Gingham, particularly suited for garden wear. The smart collar is made of white repp and delicately colored linene. Jaunty black repp tie. The piping on the three-quarter length sleeves, around the waist-line and on the deep patch pocket, is of colored linene to match the trimming on the collar. Wide skirt. Closes through in front with pearl buttons. *Colors:* black and white check, or blue and white check. *Sizes:* 32 to 46 bust; skirt length 40 inches. A remarkably serviceable morning dress.............. **$1.49**

14A55 $1.19 GINGHAM

14A55—Splendid quality Novelty Checked Gingham is used for this smart morning Dress. The collar is of solid color chambray and white piqué. Note the attractive yoke in front. The Skirt is prettily gathered at the waist-line in back. Two patch pockets, trimmed to match the collar, ornament the front. Closes in front. *Colors:* blue and white, black and white, or lavender and white. *Sizes:* 32 to 46 bust; skirt length 40 inches............ **$1.19**

14A58 98¢ GINGHAM

14A57 $1.49 GINGHAM

14A56 $1.69 LINENE

14A58—A practical, serviceable Wash Dress of good Striped Gingham for house wear. The fancy shaped collar is trimmed with solid color linene and dainty white embroidery edging. The closing edge on the front of the waist is trimmed to match. Smooth-fitting skirt, wide around the bottom. Closes through in front with small pearl buttons. *Colors:* blue and white, or gray and white. *Sizes:* 32 to 46 bust; skirt length 40 inches............ **.98**

14A56 — This fashionable Dress is made of fine quality solid white and striped Linene. The deep collar, the revers and the turn-back cuffs are of white piqué edged with pretty lace. The graceful skirt has a stylish deep peplum plaited entirely around. Invisible front closing. *Colors:* Copenhagen blue and white, or rose-pink and white. *Sizes:* 32 to 46 bust; skirt length 40 inches. Striped materials are very fashionable this season.......... **$1.69**

WE DELIVER FREE BY EXPRESS AND PARCEL POST

117

14A59
$2 39
NOVELTY
VOILE

Dresses for Morning Wear

14A60—*Extra Size* Wash Dress of high grade Striped Gingham. This dress is designed in a smart tailored style. A fashion particularly suited to the stout figure. The collar, cuffs, the trimming on the convenient breast pocket and on the belt are of solid color Chambray. The skirt is prettily gathered at the waist-line in back. Closes through in front with small fancy pearl buttons. *Colors:* blue and white stripes, or gray and white stripes; each trimmed to match. *Sizes:* 39 to 53 bust; skirt length 41 inches......... **$2.19**

14A61
$1 25
GINGHAM

14A60
$2 19
GINGHAM
EXTRA SIZE
DRESS

CHAMBRAY
14A62
98¢

14A59—Dress of excellent quality novelty Voile. A dress to wear for the morning calls. The collar and turn-back cuffs are of sheer white organdie, hemstitched and finished with a dainty lace edge. The skirt is gracefully gathered around the waist-line where it is finished with the new style heading and a black velvet belt with a bow. Crosswise section of self-material around the bottom. Closes in front with black satin buttons and buttonholes. *Color:* black and white novelty pattern. *Sizes:* 32 to 46 bust; skirt length 40 inches. **$2.39**

14A61—A morning Dress of fine quality Novelty Checked Gingham. A feature of this dress is the attractive collar which is trimmed with solid color linene, pearl buttons and dainty embroidery. The cuffs are of solid color linene. The smooth-fitting skirt is trimmed with two fashionable pockets. Closes in front. *Colors:* blue and white novelty check; pink and white novelty check; or lavender and white novelty check; each trimmed to match. *Sizes:* 32 to 46 bust; skirt length 40 inches. **$1.25**

14A62—Smart Dress of Chambray. The low neck, three-quarter length sleeves and good quality Chambray make this the ideal house dress. The trimming is of Checked Gingham to harmonize. The collar is edged off with fancy silk cording and trimmed with small pearl buttons. The skirt is smooth-fitting around the hips, and has a convenient patch pocket at the side. Closes through in front. *Colors:* blue or gray. *Sizes:* 32 to 46 bust; skirt length 40 inches............. **.98**

Every Woman Knows—

the satisfaction of a well made and carefully proportioned Petticoat.

To-day, when the style of the outer garment depends so much on the fit and hang of the petticoat, it is most important that it should fit **Just Right.**

Perry-Dame Petticoats are correctly proportioned and tailored. They fit snugly at the waist and give, at the same time, the required smoothness over the hips.

The workmanship is of the highest order. The seams are securely sewn. The plackets will not rip.

Perry-Dame Petticoats are made only of those fabrics which guarantee service. Fabrics which form for the outer skirt that foundation which is so essential to the styles of to-day.

A Perry-Dame Petticoat means absolute satisfaction.

A Silveeco Petticoat for Dress Wear

11A3—Here is a Petticoat that can be readily worn with an afternoon or evening dress. It is made of "Silveeco," a rich, lustrous, closely-woven cotton material, a fabric which has the appearance and feel of genuine Taffeta Silk. There is elastic in the waist-band making it fit the figure snugly. It fastens securely at the back with a patent clasp. The deep flounce is designed with a pin-tucked section and two fashionable pointed ruffles finished off with fluted frills, as pictured. *Colors:* black, navy blue, green, Copenhagen blue or tan. *Front Lengths:* 36 to 42 inches......... **$1.79**

11A3
$1 79
Silveeco

11A1—A fashionable perfect-fitting Petticoat of "Silveeco." This is a beautiful material made of closely-woven strong cotton threads put through a certain process making it rich and lustrous. A material which has the appearance and feel of real Taffeta Silk. The effective double-ruffle flounce is cleverly pin-tucked and finished off with accordion-plaited frills. Elastic in the waist-band. Fastens with a patent clasp in back. *Colors:* black, navy blue, green or white. *Front Lengths:* 36 to 42 inches.. **$1.29**

11A2—*Extra Sizes* of Petticoat 11A1—made extra large in the waist-band and through the hips, and with draw-string instead of elastic at the waist-line. *Front Lengths:* 37 to 43 inches. Same colors as 11A1......... **$1.49**

REGULAR SIZE
11A1
$1 29

EXTRA SIZE
11A2
$1 49
Silveeco

11A6—A dollar paid for this stylish "Silveeco" Petticoat is a dollar wisely spent. "Silveeco" is a closely woven cotton fabric with a rich, lustrous finish, extremely serviceable. The smart shirred flounce is finished with a corded pin-tucked ruffle, and provided with a dust ruffle underneath. Self-adjusting waistband. *Colors:* black, navy blue or green. *Front Lengths:* 36 to 42 inches. This Silveeco Petticoat is a model especially adapted to smooth-fitting tailored skirts................. **$1.00**

SELF-ADJUSTING WAIST BAND → Silveeco 11A6 $1.00

11A7 Silveeco $1.69

SELF-ADJUSTING WAIST BAND

SELF-ADJUSTING WAIST BAND ← 11A8 $3.50 TUB SILK

SELF-ADJUSTING WAIST BAND

11A4 $2.50 SATEEN TOP TAFFETA SILK FLOUNCE

SELF-ADJUSTING WAIST BAND

11A7—There is a handsome new striped pattern shown in the material of this smart Petticoat. It is made of Striped "Silveeco"—a lustrous, closely woven cotton fabric that is extremely serviceable. The deep flounce is effectively designed with circular and finely-plaited sections, and is finished off with a fluted frill. Self-adjusting waist-band. *Color:* black background, with stripes in stylish assorted colors. **$1.69** *Front Lengths:*36 to42inches

11A8—Here is a Petticoat every smartly dressed woman should have —a fashionable Petticoat with *Serviceability.* It is made of finest quality, closely woven genuine Tub Silk, light in weight, soft and clinging. It has a stylish pin-tucked flounce with a percaline dust ruffle underneath. Self-adjusting waist-band fastened securely at the back with a patent clasp. *Colors:* Copenhagen blue, navy blue, green or black. *FrontLengths:*36to42inches **$3.50**

11A4—Richness and serviceability are combined in this Petticoat. The stylish genuine Chiffon Taffeta Silk flounce is prettily shirred and trimmed with two ruffles. The top is of lustrous, clinging Sateen, with a self-adjusting waist-band. A dust ruffle protects the flounce. Fastens at the back with a patent clasp. *Colors:* black, navy blue, green or Copenhagen blue. *Front Lengths:* 36 to 42 inches.... **$2.50**

SELF-ADJUSTING WAIST BAND ← 11A9 $1.09 FLOWERED Silveeco

SELF ADJUSTING WAIST BAND

11A5 $1.49 Silveeco

11A5—Here is a charming new-style Petticoat made of "Silveeco"—a lustrous, closely woven, very serviceable cotton fabric, with the appearance and feel of real Taffeta Silk. The flounce is attractively accordion-plaited and trimmed with fluted frills, as pictured. Elastic in the waist-band makes the petticoat adjust itself perfectly. Fastens securely at the back with a patent clasp. *Colors:* black, navy blue or green. *Front Lengths:* 36 to 42 inches................. **$1.49**

11A9—A Flowered "Silveeco" Petticoat that you can wear from season to season because it is so serviceable and has such smart style. The material is a closely woven cotton fabric with a rich, lustrous finish. It is designed with an attractive deep flounce, as pictured. Self-adjusting waist-band fastened in back with a patent clasp. *Color:* black background, with flowers in rich assorted colorings. *Front Lengths:* 36 to 42 inches. **$1.09**

11A10—This Percaline Petticoat is attractive and serviceable. The material has a rich lustre and taffeta-like rustle. The flounce is accordion-plaited, pin-tucked, and finished with an embroidered ruffle, as pictured. Draw-strings in the waist-band. *Black Only. Front Lengths:* 36 to 42 inches. This low-priced Petticoat will give you splendid wear and just the required fullness.......... .89

11A10
89¢
PERCALINE
EMB.
FLOUNCE

DRAW
STRING

SELF-ADJUSTING
WAIST BAND
11A13
$1.69
COTTON
MESSALINE

11A14—An exceptionally handsome Petticoat for dress or general wear. It is made of "Silveeco." "Silveeco" is a closely woven, lustrous cotton fabric, famous for its serviceability and for its likeness in appearance and feel to genuine Chiffon Taffeta Silk. This petticoat has a fashionable double ruffle flounce and a self-adjusting waist-band. *Colors:* black, Copenhagen blue, navy blue or green. *Front Lengths:* 36 to 42 inches.. **$1.98**

11A14
$1.98
Silveeco
SELF-
ADJUST-
ING
WAIST
BAND

11A11—A Striped Gingham Wash Petticoat for Spring and Summer wear—light in weight, cool, and very easy to launder. It has a smooth-fitting top. The attractive bias flounce is trimmed with corded pin-tucks and finished with an embroidered scalloped edge. Draw-string in the waist-band. *Colors:* blue and white stripes; or gray and white stripes. *Front Lengths:* 36 to 42 inches................. .50

DRAW
STRING

11A15—This beautiful petticoat is made of Silk Jersey and Chiffon Taffeta Silk. The fitted top is made of the Silk Jersey—a handsome quality, closely woven and very elastic. The fashionable double ruffle flounce is of the soft Chiffon Taffeta Silk protected by a serviceable underlay. *Colors:* black, or navy blue; also green top with changeable green and blue flounce. *Front Lengths:* 36 to 42 inches............... **$3.98**

11A12
$4.95
TAFFETA
SILK
SELF-
ADJUST-
ING
WAIST
BAND

FITTED
WAIST
BAND

11A12—This Petticoat is made of Chiffon Taffeta Silk of a quality that is extraordinarily rich and beautiful. The deep flounce is elaborately trimmed with corded pin-tucks and two frills arranged in scalloped effect. Elastic in the waist-band. *Colors:* black, navy blue or green; also *Changeable* blue and gold. *Front Lengths:* 36 to 42 inches............. **$4.95**

11A11
50¢
GINGHAM

11A13—This Cotton Messaline Petticoat is soft and clinging and has a high silky lustre. Double ruffle flounce and self-adjusting waist-band. *Colors:* black, navy blue, green or Copenhagen blue. *Front Lengths:* 36 to 42 inches........................... **$1.69**

↑ **11A15 $3.98**
SILK JERSEY TOP
TAFFETA SILK FLOUNCE

The ③ Tests of Perfection in Knit Underwear

1, Does it fit right?
2, Is it comfortable?
3, Will it wear?

Perry-Dame Knit Underwear answers these tests. It is proportioned so exactly and made so carefully that it fits you perfectly. It is knitted in a firm, elastic weave. It fits smoothly over the bust. There is no unnecessary fulness at the waist nor over the hips. It is just the right weight to give the most comfort and the greatest service.

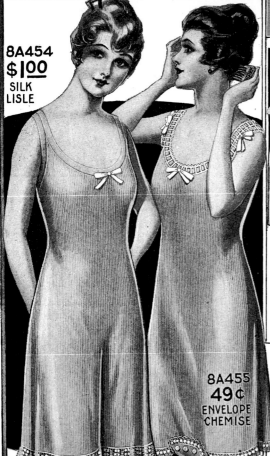

8A454 $1.00 SILK LISLE

8A455 49¢ ENVELOPE CHEMISE

8A453 $1.98 GLOVE SILK

8A452 $1.59 GLOVE SILK

8A457 29¢ **8A458 29¢**

8A457—Vest of soft White Cotton with Shirred Silk wash ribbon finishing V neck and armholes. Shoulder straps of Silk ribbon. White only. *Sizes:* 32 to 40 bust . . **.29**

8A458—Comfortable Vest of soft White Cotton with a fine Lisle finish. Neat French bands at the neck and armholes. Silk tape draw-string at the neck. "Can't-slip" shoulder straps. *Sizes:* 32 to 40 bust . . **.29**

8A459—*Extra Sizes* of Vest 8A458, 42 to 46 bust . . . . **.39**

8A452—Handsome Pure Glove Silk Vest. You will find in it real lasting service and satisfaction. The neck and armholes are edged with crocheted beading drawn with fancy silk ribbon. Reinforced under the armholes. *Colors:* flesh-pink or white. *Sizes:* 32 to 44 bust . . **$1.59**

8A453—Glove Silk Bloomer Drawers. Cut comfortably full. Double reinforced crotch. Elastic at the waist-band and knees. Closed only. *Colors:* flesh-pink or white. *Sizes:* Lengths 25 to 29 inches. Waist 20 to 30 inches **$1.98**

8A451—This beautiful Union Suit is made entirely of the finest and richest quality Glove Silk. Every thread is pure, lustrous silk that will wear splendidly and stand repeated laundering. Handsome silk embroidery adorns the front. Trim French bands at the neck and armholes are drawn with fancy silk ribbon. Reinforced under the armholes and crotch. Knee length. Open only. *Colors:* flesh-pink or white. *Sizes:* 32 to 44 bust . . **$3.69**

8A451 $3.69 EMBROIDERED GLOVE SILK

8A454—Union Suit of high grade Silk Lisle. A soft, silky fabric, knitted in a fine, elastic rib. This union suit will give comfort and excellent wear. The neck and armholes are finished with French bands, and the wide knees are edged with handsome lace. "Can't-slip" shoulder straps. Open only. *Sizes:* 32 to 40 bust **$1.00**

8A455—A light-weight Envelope Chemise of soft White close-ribbed Cotton. A garment designed for absolute comfort during the Spring and Summer months. The neck and armholes are finished with crocheted beading drawn with tape. The bottom is trimmed with pretty lace, and the flap buttons securely. *Sizes:* 32 to 40 bust. **.49**

8A456—*Extra Sizes* of Envelope Chemise 8A455, 42 to 46 bust . . . . **.55**

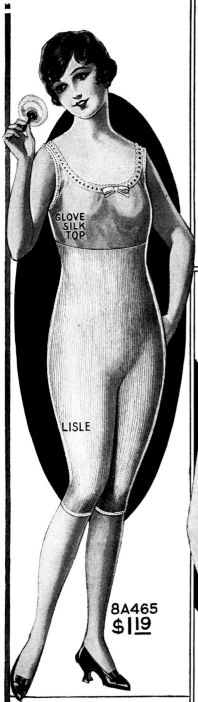

8A469 29¢

8A469—Dainty Vest of soft White Silk-striped Cotton, with "can't-slip" shoulder straps. Fine elastic rib. Crocheted silk-edged beading at the neck and armholes drawn with silk tape. *Sizes:* 32 to 40 bust... **.29**

8A468 29¢

8A468—Comfortable White Cotton Drawers with lace-trimmed wide knees. Fine rib; light weight. Muslin band. Open only. *Sizes:* 20 to 28 inches waist measure .... **.29**

8A466 19¢
8A467 25¢

8A466—A cool light-weight Vest of fine ribbed Cotton, with "can't-slip" shoulder straps. Silk ribbon at the neck. *White Sizes:* 32 to 40 bust........... **.19**

8A467—*Extra Sizes* of Vest 8A466, 42 to 46 bust. **.25**

8A465 $1.19

GLOVE SILK TOP

LISLE

Union Suit of Excellent Quality Glove Silk Combined with Finest Lisle

8A465—A Union Suit that will delight you with its comfort and rich quality. The top is made of heavy, closely-woven, lustrous Glove Silk, with mercerized beading at the neck threaded with fancy silk tape. The drawers part is made of light weight Lisle knit in a fine, elastic rib, and has close-fitting knees. Open only. *Sizes:* 32 to 40 bust. *Colors:* flesh-pink silk top or white silk top; each with White Lisle Drawers. A union suit that will give excellent service... **$1.19**

8A463 49¢
8A464 55¢

8A460 69¢
8A461 59¢
LISLE

SILK & COTTON 8A462 55¢

8A463—A band of hand-crocheted insertion trims the neck of this light-weight Cotton Union Suit which is knit in a fine, elastic rib. The wide knee-length drawers are edged with lace. Mercerized tape drawn through beading finishes the neck. Open only. *White. Sizes:* 32 to 40 bust. Will wear splendidly........ **.49**

8A464—*Extra Sizes* of Union Suit 8A463, 42 to 46 bust.................. **.55**

8A460—Fine light-weight Lisle Union Suit, with lace-trimmed wide knees and "can't-slip" shoulder straps. Silk tape at neck and armholes. You will find it delightfully comfortable and very serviceable. Open only. *Sizes:* 32 to 40 bust. (See description below for this Union Suit with close-fitting knees instead of wide knees)... **.69**

8A461—Close-fitting Knee Union Suit of fine White Lisle, same quality as 8A460. Open only. *Sizes:* 32 to 40 bust.................. **.59**

8A462—A splendid Spring and Summer Union Suit made of soft Silk-striped Cotton, woven in a fine and very elastic rib, insuring absolute comfort. It has "can't-slip" shoulder straps, a comfortable low neck threaded with mercerized tape, and wide knees edged with good quality lace. Open only. *White. Sizes:* 32 to 40 bust. The silk threads interwoven with the cotton add greatly to the serviceability and lasting shapeliness of this Union Suit............ **.55**

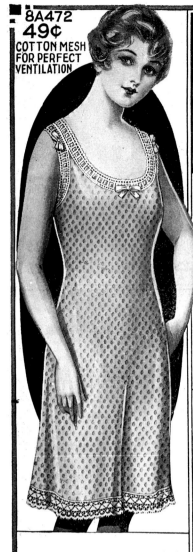

8A472
49¢
COTTON MESH
FOR PERFECT
VENTILATION

BODICE
TOP,
HIGH
GRADE
COTTON
8A473
59¢

8A476
15¢

8A476—Pretty lace-trimmed Vest of soft White Cotton, woven in a very elastic Swiss rib. Fancy beading at the neck drawn with mercerized tape to regulate the fulness. *Sizes:* 32 to 40 bust. This lace-trimmed Vest is one of the prettiest styles and of the best quality you could get anywhere for only 15 cents. **.15**

8A475—A *Closed Drawer* Union Suit with "Can't-slip" shoulder straps—a most comfortable garment in every particular. It is made of soft White Cotton, fine ribbed and very elastic. The legs are cut exceptionally wide, making the garment as convenient as an open-drawer union suit. *Sizes:* 32 to 40 bust.................... **.49**

LISLE
FINISH
COTTON
8A474
59¢

Cotton Mesh Union Suit

8A472—It is cool and sanitary, absorbing the perspiration of the body and affording perfect ventilation by means of the open mesh weave. "Can't-slip" shoulder straps. Lace-trimmed knees. Open only. *Sizes:* 32 to 40 bust.......... **.49**

8A477
12¢

8A475
49¢
CLOSED
DRAWER
UNION
SUIT

8A473—Here is the "*Bodice*" Union Suit—the newest model, just what you have wanted for a long time. It is made of fine ribbed Combed Cotton Yarn, with silk tape shoulder straps and lace-trimmed knees. Open only. *Sizes:* 32 to 40 bust. The Bodice Top makes this an ideal garment to wear with sheer waists and dresses........................ **.59**

8A474—Neat French bands with hemstitching finish the neck and armholes of this perfect-fitting Union Suit. It is made of soft Cotton with a fine Lisle finish. "Can't-slip" shoulder straps, and close-fitting knees. This garment is tailor made throughout, insuring satisfaction. Open only. *Colors:* flesh-pink or white. *Sizes:* 32 to 40 bust.......... **.59**

8A470-33¢
8A471-29¢

8A470—Union Suit with wide lace-trimmed knees, made of soft White Cotton in an elastic rib. The neck and armholes are finished with fancy beading drawn with mercerized tape. Open only. *Sizes:* 32 to 40 bust. **.33**

8A471—Close-fitting knee Union Suit of soft White Cotton, same quality as 8A470. Open only. *Sizes:* 32 to 40 bust......... **.29**

8A477—"Can't-slip" shoulder straps are a very comfortable feature. That is why you will like this Vest especially well. It is made of Swiss ribbed soft White Cotton, with "Can't-slip" shoulder straps, and mercerized beading at the neck and armholes drawn with tape. *Sizes:* 32 to 40 bust......... **.12**

A Convenient INDEX to the Garments Shown in this Catalogue

A Few Simple Directions for Ordering

Perry-Dame Clothes always fit you perfectly if you order the right size garment. And it is a very easy matter for you to find out just what size garment you should wear—that is by actually taking your measurement with an accurate tape measure.

To find your correct BUST MEASURE, take an accurate tape measure and your size will be the number of inches over the largest part of bust, taken over your shirtwaist. Be sure that the tape measure does not slip up or down in the back, and do not take this measurement too tight. Make no allowances whatever.

To find your correct WAIST MEASURE, take this measurement all around your waist, making no allowances.

To find your correct HIP MEASURE, take this measurement all around your hips about six inches below your waist line, making no allowances.

When ordering SKIRTS, whether with a regulation waist band or girdle top, give your waist measure taken around your waist, making no allowances; and also give front length, taken from waist line to desired length. See diagram on page 146.

Read how to order your right size Dress on page 12 or 146
Read how to order your right size Coat on page 53 or 146
Read how to order your right size Suit on page 77 or 146
Read how to order your right size Corset on page 87
Read how to order your right size Shoes on page 91
Read how to order your right size Gloves on page 146

Here Are Two Special Value Pages

We have not tried to show cheap merchandise on these pages but GOOD MERCHANDISE—MERCHANDISE THAT EVERYBODY WANTS AND MERCHANDISE THAT EVERYBODY NEEDS at prices that EVERYBODY CAN AFFORD.

PERRY, DAME & COMPANY have established a high standard of quality. We have maintained that high standard in these pages.

Look over the articles here shown—remember that you can't match these values anywhere—then send us your order.

You will be pleased that you made the purchase. Our GUARANTEE applies to all the goods we show.

(Read our Guarantee on page 2 inside front cover)

Serviceable Sport Middy

9A54—An Unusually Low Priced Middy of Specially Good Galatea. The tiny breast pocket, the cuffs and the smooth setting round collar are of striped linene in blue and white or pink and white. The collar is neatly finished with a narrow piping of white linene. The front lacing is effected through securely stitched buttonholes with mercerized laces, and here a piping of the striped material is effectively introduced. *Sizes:* 32 to 42 bust measure..........................**.59**

5A46
$2.⁷⁹

9A54
59c

A Sport Skirt of Exceptional Value

5A46—Carefully Tailored Sport Skirt of firmly woven Black and White Shepherd Check. The price is *exceptionally* moderate. Especially when you take into consideration the quality of the material and the neat and workmanlike manner in which every seam is stitched. Patch pockets trimmed with bone buttons to match those which appear on the overlapping front seam. The well-shaped belt is cut in yoke outline and is finished with two deep points in front. The back of skirt is cut on smart plain tailored lines. *Sizes:* 22 to 30 inches waist measure. Lengths: 36 to 43 inches..............**$2.79**

5A47—Same material and colors but in small women's and misses' sizes: Waist 22 to 28 inches. Lengths: 33 to 35 inches..**$2.79**

Sport Coat of Unusual Value

3A32—Fine Spring and Summer Sport Coat of Black and White Honeycomb Cloth. An excellent material for spring and summer wear. Deep front facing. Every seam securely bound. Latest style details: Deep square collar with a band of figured Silk. The collar can be worn rever fashion or buttoned close to throat; cross strap belt at front; deep patch pockets; turned-back cuffs; novelty button trimming. *Colors:* Black and white plaid. *Sizes:* 32 to 46 bust measure. Length 35 inches..........**$4.98**

3A32
**$4**$\underline{98}$

Excellent Value Tailored Hat
7A55
98c

7A55—Patent Milan Hat of excellent quality. Neat and serviceable for every day wear. Well made throughout and finished with an inside lining. The side crown is trimmed with a band of matching colored velvet which terminates at the front in a smart rosette with slashed end and straw buckle center. *Colors:* Copenhagen, old rose, emerald green, national blue or cardinal red, all with white top crown and white straw buckle......**.98**

A Specially Priced Sport Hat

7A54—"Crush" or Folding Pocket Hat for Sport or General Wear. It is made of Linen Finished Etamine Cloth. Stitched brim. Four-quarter crown. Band of the material. Inside band and a loosely woven, cool lining. *Colors:* White, Copenhagen, old rose, apple green or gold. An exceptional value..........**.49**

7A54
49c

6A130

A Perry Dame Special Bargain

6A130—A Black Vici Kid Oxford with flexible cushion inner sole. Comfortable round toe with fine Patent Leather Tip. Low heel with rubber top lift. *Sizes:* 2½ to 9. Widths: D, E and EE...**$1.98**

A Money Saving Opportunity

6A131—Black Canvas "Juliette" Slippers. Patent Leather Tips. Full round toe. Elastic side gores and low rubber heels. *Sizes:* 2½ to 8. Widths: E, EE and EEE.**$1.20**

6A131

THE HOME OF PERRY, DAME & CO.
IN NEW YORK CITY

We Sell by Mail, Women's, Misses' and Children's Wearing Apparel Only

YOUR FRIENDS who have not received one of these catalogues should have one. Won't you help us get one to them?

Perry, Dame & Company depend entirely for their large business upon the values they give, the beauty of the styles they show, the excellence of the materials and thoroughness of the workmanship which enter into their merchandise.

For the continued increase of their already big business, they depend upon the friendship of their customers. Perry, Dame & Company want to merit that friendship by giving their customers the fairest treatment possible and a little better service than anyone else can give.

If you will show this catalogue to your friend or neighbor we believe you will be doing her a favor—if you will ask Her to Write Us Direct asking for a catalogue like yours, you will most certainly do us a great favor.

We want to thank you now for recommending us to your friends.

Yours very truly,

Perry, Dame & Co.

LADIES' FINE QUALITY SILK AND COTTON HOSIERY

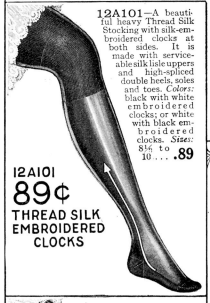

12A101—A beautiful heavy Thread Silk Stocking with silk-embroidered clocks at both sides. It is made with serviceable silk lisle uppers and high-spliced double heels, soles and toes. *Colors:* black with white embroidered clocks; or white with black embroidered clocks. *Sizes:* 8½ to 10 89

12A101
89¢
THREAD SILK EMBROIDERED CLOCKS

EVERY STOCKING IS A BARGAIN. PERFECT IN FIT, STYLE, COMFORT AND WEARING QUALITIES. NO COARSE SEAMS TO HURT THE FEET. SATISFACTORY IN EVERY WAY.

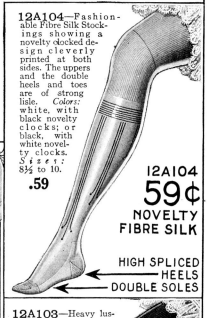

12A104—Fashionable Fibre Silk Stockings showing a novelty clocked design cleverly printed at both sides. The uppers and the double heels and toes are of strong lisle. *Colors:* white, with black novelty clocks; or black, with white novelty clocks. *Sizes:* 8½ to 10. **.59**

12A104
59¢
NOVELTY FIBRE SILK

HIGH SPLICED HEELS
DOUBLE SOLES

This Thread Silk Full-Fashioned Hose Is Guaranteed To Give Good Service

12A100
$1.19

Silk Stockings of Exceptional Quality

12A100—Exceedingly rich, perfect-fitting, and *guaranteed* for service are these handsome Stockings. They are made of heavy, all-Silk threads, very closely woven. They are full fashioned, and have double high-spliced heels, soles and toes. Fine Silk Lisle double garter tops. *Colors:* black, white, navy blue, bronze or gray. *Sizes:* 8½ to 10. These handsome Silk Stockings are *guaranteed* to give you perfect service. Just the stockings for those new evening slippers **$1.19**

12A102—Fibre Silk Stockings with unusual richness and service-giving qualities. Double reinforced garter tops of strong lisle. Double heels, soles and toes. *Colors:* black or white. *Sizes:* 8½ to 10. These Fibre Silk Stockings will wear like iron . . **.55**

12A102
55¢
FIBRE SILK REINFORCED

DOUBLE HEELS
SOLES
AND TOES

12A103—Heavy lustrous quality Thread Silk is used for this handsome dress stocking. It is a quality suitable for all dress occasions. Fine gauge uppers of Silk Lisle. *Colors:* black, white, navy blue or bronze. *Sizes:* 8½ to 10. **.89**

FINE GAUGE SILK LISLE TOP

12A103
89¢
THREAD SILK SEAMLESS

HIGH SPLICED HEELS
DOUBLE SOLES

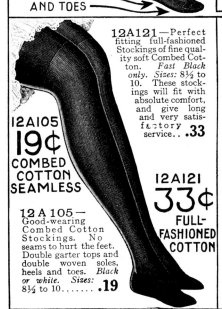

12A105
19¢
COMBED COTTON SEAMLESS

12A105—Good-wearing Combed Cotton Stockings. No seams to hurt the feet. Double garter tops and double woven soles, heels and toes. *Black or white. Sizes:* 8½ to 10 . . . . . . **.19**

12A121—Perfect fitting full-fashioned Stockings of fine quality soft Combed Cotton. *Fast Black only. Sizes:* 8½ to 10. These stockings will fit with absolute comfort, and give long and very satisfactory service . . **.33**

12A121
33¢
FULL-FASHIONED COTTON

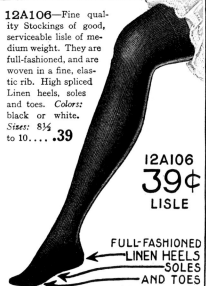

12A106—Fine quality Stockings of good, serviceable lisle of medium weight. They are full-fashioned, and are woven in a fine, elastic rib. High spliced Linen heels, soles and toes. *Colors:* black or white. *Sizes:* 8½ to 10 . . . . **.39**

12A106
39¢
LISLE

FULL-FASHIONED
LINEN HEELS
SOLES
AND TOES

12A107—A splendid-wearing Stocking made of Silk Lisle. It has a fine and very elastic weave. It is full seamless, and the heels, soles and toes are made double, insuring extra service. Double garter tops. *Colors:* black, white or tan. *Sizes:* 8½ to 10. **.29**

12A107
29¢
SILK LISLE FULL SEAMLESS

DOUBLE HEELS
SOLES
AND TOES

SEE OUR GUARANTEE ON PAGE 2

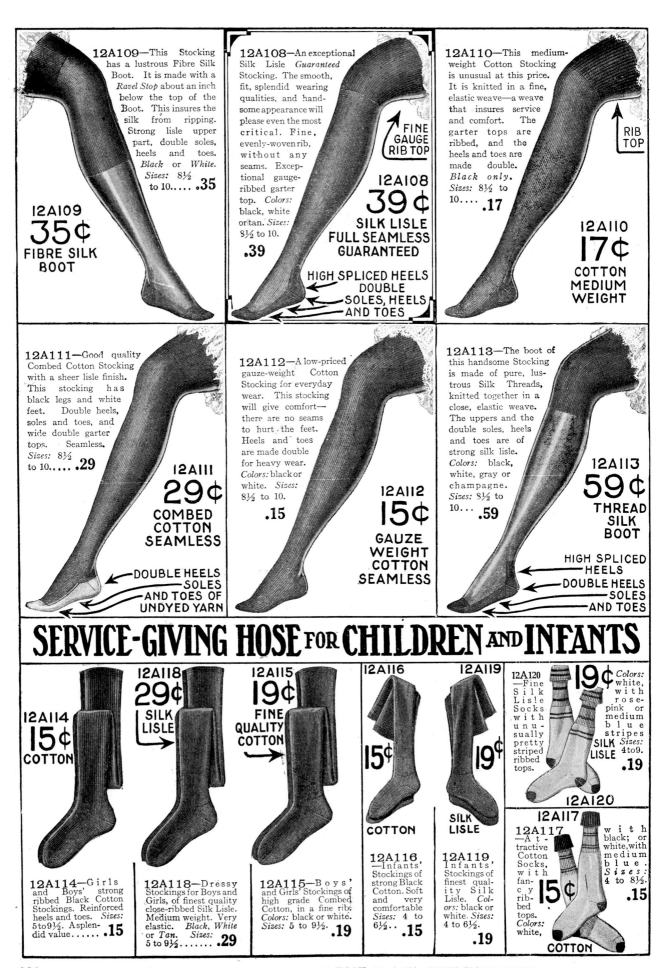

12A109—This Stocking has a lustrous Fibre Silk Boot. It is made with a *Ravel Stop* about an inch below the top of the Boot. This insures the silk from ripping. Strong lisle upper part, double soles, heels and toes. *Black or White. Sizes: 8½ to 10.....* **.35**

12A109
35¢
FIBRE SILK BOOT

12A108—An exceptional Silk Lisle *Guaranteed* Stocking. The smooth, fit, splendid wearing qualities, and handsome appearance will please even the most critical. Fine, evenly-woven rib, without any seams. Exceptional gauge-ribbed garter top. *Colors:* black, white or tan. *Sizes:* 8½ to 10.

FINE GAUGE RIB TOP

12A108
39¢
SILK LISLE FULL SEAMLESS GUARANTEED

.39

HIGH SPLICED HEELS DOUBLE SOLES, HEELS AND TOES

12A110—This medium-weight Cotton Stocking is unusual at this price. It is knitted in a fine, elastic weave—a weave that insures service and comfort. The garter tops are ribbed, and the heels and toes are made double. *Black only. Sizes: 8½ to 10....* **.17**

RIB TOP

12A110
17¢
COTTON MEDIUM WEIGHT

12A111—Good quality Combed Cotton Stocking with a sheer lisle finish. This stocking has black legs and white feet. Double heels, soles and toes, and wide double garter tops. *Seamless. Sizes:* 8½ to 10..... **.29**

12A111
29¢
COMBED COTTON SEAMLESS

DOUBLE HEELS SOLES AND TOES OF UNDYED YARN

12A112—A low-priced gauze-weight Cotton Stocking for everyday wear. This stocking will give comfort— there are no seams to hurt the feet. Heels and toes are made double for heavy wear. *Colors:* black or white. *Sizes:* 8½ to 10.

12A112
15¢
GAUZE WEIGHT COTTON SEAMLESS

.15

12A113—The boot of this handsome Stocking is made of pure, lustrous Silk Threads, knitted together in a close, elastic weave. The uppers and the double soles, heels and toes are of strong silk lisle. *Colors:* black, white, gray or champagne. *Sizes:* 8½ to 10... **.59**

12A113
59¢
THREAD SILK BOOT

HIGH SPLICED HEELS DOUBLE HEELS SOLES AND TOES

SERVICE-GIVING HOSE FOR CHILDREN AND INFANTS

12A114
15¢
COTTON

12A118
29¢
SILK LISLE

12A115
19¢
FINE QUALITY COTTON

15¢
COTTON

12A116

12A119
19¢
SILK LISLE

12A120—Fine Silk Lisle Socks with unusually pretty striped ribbed tops.

19¢
Colors: white, with rose-pink or medium blue stripes *Sizes:* 4 to 9.
SILK LISLE
.19

12A120

12A117—Attractive Cotton Socks, with fancy ribbed tops. *Colors:* white,

15¢

with black; or white, with medium blue *Sizes:* 4 to 8½.
.15

12A117

COTTON

12A114—Girls and Boys' strong ribbed Black Cotton Stockings. Reinforced heels and toes. *Sizes:* 5 to 9½. A splendid value...... **.15**

12A118—Dressy Stockings for Boys and Girls, of finest quality close-ribbed Silk Lisle. Medium weight. Very elastic. *Black, White or Tan. Sizes:* 5 to 9½....... **.29**

12A115—Boys' and Girls' Stockings of high grade Combed Cotton, in a fine rib. *Colors:* black or white. *Sizes:* 5 to 9½. **.19**

12A116, Infants' Stockings of strong Black Cotton. Soft and very comfortable *Sizes:* 4 to 6½.. **.15**

12A119, Infants' Stockings of finest quality Silk Lisle. *Colors:* black or white. *Sizes:* 4 to 6½. **.19**

The New "Beverly" Princess Slip

8A4—It is made of fine quality soft White Nainsook. Effectively trimmed on the front bodice and deep flounce with fine Val lace, insertion, and sheer embroidered organdie. Silk ribbon at the neck controls the fulness and adds a dainty touch. Closes in front. *Sizes: 32 to 46 bust.* Will show up beautifully any dress or shirtwaist and skirt that you wear over it....... **$1.69**

A Handsome New Style Princess Slip

8A2—It is made of high grade soft White Nainsook. The exquisite front bodice is composed of embroidered organdie and exquisite Art lace, set off with lustrous silk ribbons. Little lace cap sleeves. The handsome flounce matches the bodice. Closes in front. *Sizes: 32 to 46 bust.* A remarkably beautiful Princess Slip with individuality. **$2.29**

8A1 $1.98

8A3 $1.00

8A5 $1.29

8A4 $1.69

8A2 $2.29

Exquisite White Nainsook Princess Slip

8A1—This fine Slip is trimmed with rows and rows of a strong handsome combination of Val and Filet pattern laces. The front "Princess Bodice" is finished off with pointed Filet pattern lace and ribbon run beading, as pictured, and the deep flounce is made to match. Closes in front. *Sizes: 32 to 46 bust......* **$1.98**

One-Piece Corset Cover and Petticoat Slip

8A3—It is a perfect-fitting garment, made of fine quality soft White Muslin and attractive embroidery. The front of the cover and the deep flounce are made of the embroidery, as pictured. Silk ribbon controls the fulness at the neck and waistline. Closes in front. *Sizes: 32 to 46 bust.* A splendid bargain... **$1.00**

The "Gloria" Princess Slip

8A5—It is a very fashionable White Nainsook model. This Slip is trimmed with handsome Filet pattern lace which is an extremely popular trimming. The front bodice with cap sleeves is made of the lace, set off by ribbon-run beading. The flounce is made to match. Silk ribbon controls the fulness at the neck and provides a charming finishing touch. Closes in front. *Sizes: 32 to 46 bust....* **$1.29**

8A12 95¢

8A6 $1.29

8A9 $4.98 Silk Crepe de Chine

Women's Dainty Nightgowns

8A12—A fine quality soft-finished Cambric Gown. Insertions of lace and two embroidered organdie medallions form the yoke of this attractive Gown. The sleeves are edged with lace. Wash silk ribbon controls the fulness at the neck. *White. Sizes: 32 to 46 bust* . . . .**.95**

8A6—A dainty Gown of fine quality soft-finished Muslin. The charming trimming consists of lace, embroidered organdie, a section of tucked Nainsook and a French satin ribbon rosette, as pictured. *White. Sizes: 32 to 46 bust.* A gown which combines beauty with comfort **$1.29**

8A9—This is a perfectly lovely Silk Crêpe de Chine Gown—dainty, rich and charmingly trimmed! You will say so, too, when you see it. It is made of fine quality lustrous, closely-woven Silk Crêpe de Chine in a delicate flesh-pink. It has an exquisitely dainty bodice, front and back alike. The broad shoulder straps are made of fine Shadow Lace threaded at each side with heavy satin ribbon. *Sizes: 32 to 46 bust.* The most beautiful Silk Crêpe de Chine Gown ever bought for **$4.98**

Cap 8A153 29¢

8A10 $1.29

8A11 $1.98

8A7 $1.19

8A8 $1.00

8A11—"The Geneva" Gown—dainty, cool and richly trimmed. It is made of fine quality soft Nainsook, with a graceful V-shape neck of exquisite Point de Paris lace, front and back alike. Silk ribbon at the neck. Embroidered organdie and sections of lace further trim the front and sleeves, as pictured. *White. Sizes: 32 to 46 bust.* **$1.98**
8A153—Boudoir Hood of rich Silk Brocade trimmed with shadow lace and a ribbon bow. Gathered on an elastic band. *Colors: pink or light blue.* . . . .**.29**

8A10—The material in this Gown is an exceptional quality soft White Crinkled Crêpe. The floral design shows the charming color-combination of blue and pink. It is prettily trimmed with lace, silk ribbon and shirrings, *Sizes: 32 to 46 bust.* Washes beautifully and requires no ironing. **$1.29**

8A8—Gown of fine quality soft White Longcloth trimmed with beautiful and very strong embroidery. The dainty Empire yoke is set off with embroidery beading run with wide silk ribbon ending in a bow. *White. Sizes: 32 to 46 bust.* Will give excellent service. **$1.00**

8A7—This charming Gown of soft-finished Muslin for only $1.19! It is richly trimmed across the front with Point de Paris and Shadow laces, and finished with silk ribbons. *White. Sizes: 32 to 46 bust.* The stylish Empire Yoke is finished with Van Dyke points of Shadow Lace **$1.19**

8A19 $2⁰⁰ Silk Crêpe de Chine Top

Cap **8A15I 59¢**

8A16 $1.19

8A15 $1⁰⁰

Flesh Color Batiste

8A14 59¢

8A20 $1.25

8A18 79¢

8A17 $1.25

8A15—*An extremely desirable selection.* This gown is of soft White Nainsook. It has a charming V-neck Empire yoke of embroidery, lace and embroidered organdie, as pictured. The yoke is set off with ribbon-run beading. *Sizes:* 32 to 46 bust. **$1.00**

8A19—A beautiful Gown of flesh-pink Silk-finished Batiste. This gown has a handsome lustrous Silk Crêpe de Chine bodice. It is trimmed with lace and a dainty French blue satin ribbon rosette. *Sizes:* 32 to 46 bust. There is charming simplicity in this dainty Gown.................... **$2.00**

8A151—China Silk Boudoir Cap trimmed with White Point d'esprit Lace, and chiffon rosebuds with leaves. *Colors:* pink or light blue.......... **.59**

8A16—Here is a cool and pretty Gown of good quality soft White Nainsook. It is trimmed with insertions of lace and a section of sheer embroidered organdie set off with lace in scalloped outline. The fulness at the neck is controlled by lustrous silk ribbon. *Sizes:* 32 to 46 bust. This is one of those soft, pretty gowns that is always so delightfully comfortable and cool........ **$1.19**

8A14—A splendid Gown, serviceable and pretty. The material is a good quality soft-finished Cambric. It is attractively trimmed with scalloped embroidery run with wash silk ribbon. The sleeves are finished with scalloped edging. *White*. *Sizes:* 32 to 46 bust. An unusual gown for the price.....**59**

8A20—Four dainty Shadow Lace butterflies with lustrous satin ribbon underneath trim this lovely soft White Nainsook Gown. The upper part of the yoke is made of bands of lace and nainsook. Silk ribbon at the neck controls the fulness. *Sizes:* 32 to 46 bust. You will surely be delighted with the richness of this Gown............. **$1.25**

8A18—Slipover Gown of good, serviceable Muslin, with a comfortable round neck and short sleeves. It is made with gathers at the yoke, and is trimmed with sheer embroidered organdie and lace. Wash silk ribbon at the neck. *White.* *Sizes:* 32 to 46 bust. This is an unusually pretty and dainty gown for such a low price.................. **.79**

8A17—This soft White Nainsook Gown is made unusually beautiful by the sections of heavily embroidered organdie which trim the front. Lace insertion and edging and lustrous silk ribbon add to its richness. *Sizes:* 32 to 46 bust. There is service in this gown as well as beauty. It will always launder fresh and snowy white............. **$1.25**

Cap
8A154
39¢

8A25
$1.49

8A24
$1.59

8A23
$1.29

A Gown of Exceptional Beauty

8A25—The body of this gown is made of fine quality soft White Nainsook. The lace which trims the front and back of this exquisite Gown and also forms the sleeves is Point de Paris lace—rich and dainty, and very serviceable. Lustrous wash silk ribbon drawn through the lace adds further to its wondrous beauty. *Sizes:* 32 to 46 bust...................... **$1.49**

8A22
79¢

8A24—Exceptionally dainty Empire Gown of fine quality soft White Nainsook. The yoke is made of fine embroidery in a handsome solid and openwork pattern. Ribbon-run beading and lace finish the yoke, as pictured. *Sizes:* 32 to 46 bust.......... **$1.59**

8A154—Boudoir Cap of Silk Crêpe de Chine and White Shadow Lace, gathered on an elastic band. Trimmed with a fancy ornament. *Colors:* pink or light blue.**39**

8A23—The arrangement of the trimming on this soft White Nainsook Gown is perfectly beautiful. Bands of lace joined together with a scroll design of lace insertion and embroidered organdie medallions form the yoke and sleeves. Ribbon rosette at each side of the front. *Sizes:* 32 to 46 bust. The fineness of this gown will appeal strongly to all... **$1.29**

8A27
95¢

8A28
89¢

8A26
69¢

8A27—The ribbon-run Embroidered Organdie and Laces used to trim this Gown are responsible for its daintiness. The body of this pretty gown is of high grade White Nainsook. The yoke is finished at the bottom with a row of Val lace giving the popular Empire effect. *Sizes:* 32 to 46 bust............ **.95**

8A22—This attractive Slipover Gown of fine quality Crinkled Crêpe is trimmed with Japanese embroidery and Smocking. The neck and sleeves are embroidered in scalloped outline. The neck and sleeves are embroidered in scalloped outline. *Colors:* white, with embroidery in pink or light blue, as preferred. *Sizes:* 32 to 46 bust. An ideal warm weather gown. It washes beautifully and requires no ironing............ **.79**

8A28—Serviceable Open-front Gown made of fine quality soft-finished Muslin. It has an embroidery front-yoke in a solid and openwork design of unusual beauty. Clusters of pin tucks further trim the yoke. Ribbon bow at the neck, and embroidery edging on the three-quarter length sleeves. *White. Sizes:* 32 to 46 bust................. **.89**

8A26—Cool Gown of good quality soft-finished Cambric. The sleeves are lace-edged. The attractive yoke is made of lace insertion and a band of embroidered organdie. The round neck, which is threaded with ribbon, is also edged with lace. *White. Sizes:* 32 to 46 bust. Excellent value. **.69**

Serviceable Nightgowns for Women

8A32—This exquisite Nainsook Gown is one of the season's latest models. Trimmed with the daintiest of Val laces and Embroidered Organdie medallions, as well as satin ribbon, narrow shirrings and silk crêpe de chine rosebuds. *White. Sizes: 32 to 46 bust.* **$2.19**

8A34—New style "Bodice" Gown of soft White Nainsook, charmingly trimmed with Filet pattern lace and lustrous satin ribbon bows. *Sizes: 32 to 46 bust.* **$1.29**

8A152—Boudoir Cap of White Shadow Lace and beautiful quality Satin Ribbon in *Pink* or *Light Blue*, as preferred. **.59**

8A31
$1.25
Flesh Color Batiste Hand Embroidered

8A31—Empire Gown of Flesh-pink Silk-finished Batiste, with hand embroidered flowers in natural colors. The neck and sleeves are edged with lace. Silk ribbon controls the fulness at the neck and provides a dainty finishing touch. *Sizes: 32 to 46 bust.* If you love dainty lingerie, by all means order this charming Gown. (Matches Envelope Chemise No. 8A52 shown on Page 138) **$1.25**

Cap 8A152 59¢

8A32 $2.19

8A34 $1.29

8A30 69¢

8A33 $1.00

8A29—This new-style Slipover Gown of soft White Muslin is light in weight and very comfortable. It is trimmed with pink hemstitching, and fastens with two white braid frogs and pearl buttons. *Sizes: 32 to 46 bust.* Here is a gown that will stand the wear and tear of repeated launderings because of its serviceable quality and practical style. **.65**

8A35—Neat and serviceable Gown made of soft-finished Cambric. Round neck and little cap sleeves edged with lace. Attractive yoke of embroidery outlined with Filet pattern insertion. *White. Sizes: 32 to 46 bust.* The good quality Cambric and the strong embroidery and lace trimmings used in this Gown will give most satisfactory service. **.79**

8A29 65¢

8A35 79¢

8A30—Comfortable Open-front Gown of durable White Muslin, with an attractive front yoke of eyelet embroidery and pin-tucks. Reinforced double back yoke of self-material. The neck and long sleeves are finished off with embroidered scalloped edging. *Sizes: 32 to 46 bust.* A 69 cent gown of quality that will please you and that will give good service. **.69**

8A33—Gown of good quality soft White Nainsook, Filet lace and panels of sheer embroidered organdie trim this Gown beautifully, while silk ribbon drawn through the lace at the neck controls the fulness and adds a dainty touch. *Sizes: 32 to 46 bust.* Filet lace is used a great deal on the finest underwear this season, and in this gown there is an unusually beautiful pattern. **$1.00**

SATISFACTION GUARANTEED OR YOUR MONEY REFUNDED

135

Combinations Moderately Priced

8A40—The Bodice of this lovely Nainsook Envelope Chemise is beautifully designed front and back of embroidered organdie. It has the finest Shadow lace, Val insertion and edging. Val insertion and edging also trim the bottom, as pictured. Silk ribbon at the neck, tying in a pretty bow. *White.* *Sizes: 32 to 46 bust* **$1.98**

8A38
$1.25

8A40
$1.98

8A42
$2.59
Silk Crepe de Chine

8A38—This Envelope Chemise is made of excellent quality Nainsook. It is beautifully trimmed with lace, embroidered organdie panels and silk ribbon, as pictured. A pretty finish is given by the extra insertion of lace near the lower edge. *White. Sizes: 32 to 46 bust* **$1.25**

8A42—An exquisite Silk Crepe de Chine Envelope Chemise, Crepe de Chine is much in demand this season. It is trimmed entirely around the top and the bottom with finest Val and Shadow lace. Silk ribbon and chiffon rosebuds at the neck. *Color:* flesh-pink. *Sizes: 32 to 46 bust* **$2.59**

8A39
69¢

8A41
98¢

8A43
59¢

8A39—Very serviceable and comfortable Envelope Chemise of good quality soft-finished Cambric, prettily trimmed with lace. The V-shape neck is threaded with silk ribbon tying in a bow. *White. Sizes: 32 to 46 bust* .... **.69**

8A41—The dainty lace cap-sleeves on this soft Nainsook Envelope Chemise make it a very desirable piece of underwear. The attractive yoke is made of lace, fine eyelet embroidery and silk ribbon. *White. Sizes: 32 to 46 bust* .... **.98**

8A43—Unusually pretty Envelope Chemise of good quality Muslin, trimmed with lace and embroidered organdie in an attractive design. Silk ribbon at the neck. *White. Sizes: 32 to 46 bust.* This Envelope Chemise is a decided bargain .... **.59**

8A47 69¢

8A46 89¢

8A47—This Crinkled Crêpe Envelope Chemise is delightful to wear and easy to launder, requiring no ironing. Lace trims the neck, armholes and the lower edge. Wash silk ribbon adds a dainty touch. *White.* *Sizes:* 32 to 46 bust.......................**.69**

8A46—A pretty Empire style Envelope Chemise of soft White Cambric. It has an attractive yoke of ribbon-run embroidered organdie, lace and ribbon-run beading. Lace edging around the bottom. *White.* *Sizes:* 32 to 46 bust.......................**.89**

8A48 $1.89

8A48—A perfectly charming new style is shown in this "Bodice" Envelope Chemise. The material and trimmings are as fine as could be desired. It is made of soft Nainsook, trimmed with exquisite Point de Paris lace forming a pretty V at the neck in front and also in back. Silk ribbon bows on the shoulders and in front. *White Sizes:* 32 to 46 bust.................... **$1.89**

8A45 $1.25

8A44 98¢

8A49 89¢

8A45—The trimming around the entire upper part of this Nainsook Envelope Chemise is exceptionally dainty and pretty. It consists of rows of Filet pattern lace, China Silk and embroidered organdie. The shoulder straps are of Filet pattern lace, and there is an attractive French ribbon-rosette on the front of the bodice, as pictured. **$1.25** *White.* *Sizes:* 32 to 46 bust..

8A44—Lace insertion, lace edging and scalloped embroidery of an unusually handsome design trim this Envelope Chemise of soft White Longcloth. Lace insertion outlines the yoke in scalloped effect. The neck is run with dainty silk ribbon tying in a bow. *Sizes:* 32 to 46 bust. This Envelope Chemise will wear splendidly, and you will find it most comfortable.............**.98**

8A49—You will be delighted with the rich style and excellent value of this Envelope Chemise. It is made of soft-finished Cambric in the beautiful Empire style so fashionable this season. Lace, and organdie handsomely embroidered with Japanese floss in a raised floral design form the dainty front yoke. *White.* *Sizes:* 32 to 46 bust........**.89**

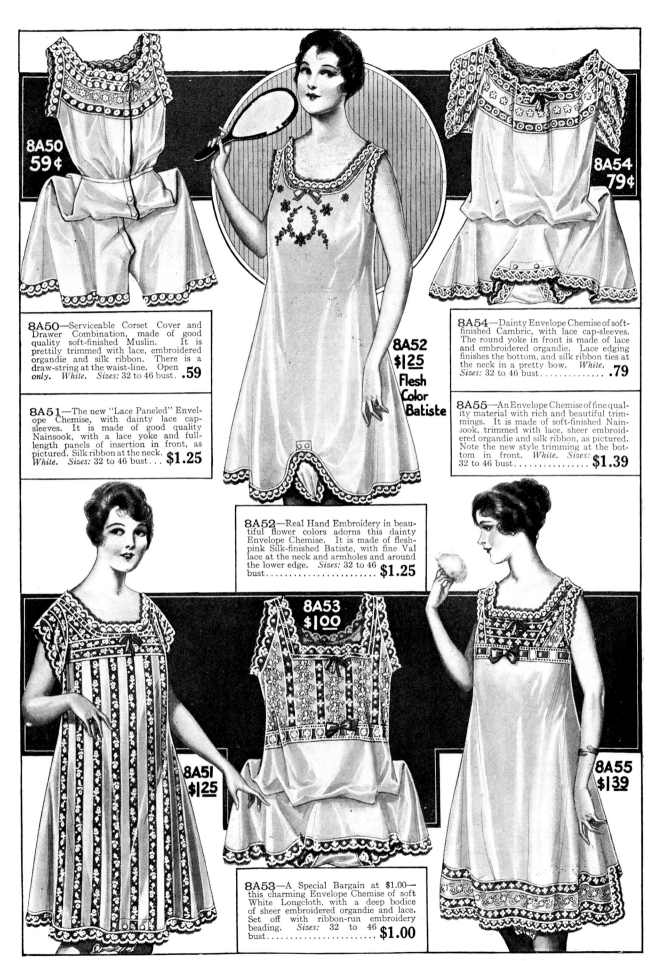

8A50
59¢

8A54
79¢

8A52
$1.25
Flesh
Color
Batiste

8A50—Serviceable Corset Cover and Drawer Combination, made of good quality soft-finished Muslin. It is prettily trimmed with lace, embroidered organdie and silk ribbon. There is a draw-string at the waist-line. Open only. White. Sizes: 32 to 46 bust. **.59**

8A51—The new "Lace Paneled" Envelope Chemise, with dainty lace cap-sleeves. It is made of good quality Nainsook, with a lace yoke and full-length panels of insertion in front, as pictured. Silk ribbon at the neck. White. Sizes: 32 to 46 bust... **$1.25**

8A54—Dainty Envelope Chemise of soft-finished Cambric, with lace cap-sleeves. The round yoke in front is made of lace and embroidered organdie. Lace edging finishes the bottom, and silk ribbon ties at the neck in a pretty bow. White. Sizes: 32 to 46 bust.............. **.79**

8A55—An Envelope Chemise of fine quality material with rich and beautiful trimmings. It is made of soft-finished Nainsook, trimmed with lace, sheer embroidered organdie and silk ribbon, as pictured. Note the new style trimming at the bottom in front. White. Sizes: 32 to 46 bust............... **$1.39**

8A52—Real Hand Embroidery in beautiful flower colors adorns this dainty Envelope Chemise. It is made of flesh-pink Silk-finished Batiste, with fine Val lace at the neck and armholes and around the lower edge. Sizes: 32 to 46 bust....................... **$1.25**

8A53
$1.00

8A51
$1.25

8A55
$1.39

8A53—A Special Bargain at $1.00—this charming Envelope Chemise of soft White Longcloth, with a deep bodice of sheer embroidered organdie and lace. Set off with ribbon-run embroidery beading. Sizes: 32 to 46 bust....................... **$1.00**

Women's Drawers

8A60 **59¢** Envelope Drawer

8A56—Serviceable Cambric Drawers trimmed with pin-tucks and attractive scalloped edge embroidery. Open or closed. *Sizes:* 23 to 27 inches Side Length...... .29

8A56 **29¢**

8A60—Nainsook Envelope Drawers trimmed with Val lace. Perfect-fitting at the waist-line and over the hips. Draw-string in the waist-band, tying in back. *Sizes:* 23 to 27 inches Side Length. Delightfully comfortable....... .59

8A64 **59¢**

8A65—Thin, comfortable Drawers of fine quality Crinkled Crepe. Wide knees trimmed with lace. Open or closed. *Sizes:* 23 to 27 inches Side Length. Wash splendidly and require no ironing.............................. .39

8A65 **39¢**

8A64—Handsome ribbon-run embroidery trims these Drawers. They are made of fine quality soft-finished Muslin and are perfectly proportioned. Open or closed. *Sizes:* 23 to 27 inches Side Length.................. .59

8A61 **39¢**

8A57—Fine Nainsook Drawers trimmed with Baby Irish Crochet Pattern Lace. The lace is threaded with silk ribbon tying in dainty bows. Open or closed. *Sizes:* 23 to 27 inches Side Length........................... .69

8A57 **69¢**

8A61—Perfect-fitting Drawers of fine quality Muslin. The rich ruffles are headed with pin-tucks, as pictured. Open or closed. *Sizes:* 23 to 27 inches Side Length......................... .39

8A59 **98¢**

8A59—Corset Cover and Drawer Combination of rich Lawn Embroidery. The back of the cover is of fine Muslin. Open only. *Sizes:* 32 to 46 bust..................... .98

8A58 **49¢**

8A62 **59¢**

8A63 **49¢** Extra Size

8A58—Attractive embroidery ruffles trim these Drawers. They are made of fine quality Muslin with pin-tucks above the embroidery. Open or closed. *Sizes:* 23 to 27 inches Side Length.................. .49

8A62—A beautiful arrangement of Val lace and embroidered organdie medallions trims these fine Nainsook Drawers. Open or closed. *Sizes:* 23 to 27 inches Side Length................................. .59

8A63—*Extra Size* Drawers—extra large in the waist-band and through the hips. Made of Longcloth, trimmed with pin-tucks and embroidery. Open only. *Sizes:* 27 to 29 inches Side Length................ .49

SEE COMPLETE INDEX ON PAGE 125

139

8A66—This soft-finished Cambric Petticoat for only 59 cents will delight you with its quality and workmanship. It is made with an attractive embroidery flounce and a heading to match. Draw-string in the waist-band. *White. Front Lengths:* 36 to 42 inches..........................**.59**

8A68—Durable Petticoat of soft-finished Cambric. Filet lace is very stylish this season and an attractive pattern is used to trim the flounce of this Petticoat. It is combined with a section of embroidery run with silk ribbon, as pictured. Cambric underlay. *White. Front Lengths:* 36 to 42 inches........................**$1.00**

8A70—Here is a splendid Shadow-proof Petticoat of good strong Cambric for every-day wear. It is neat, well-fitting and serviceable. It has a hemstitched tucked ruffle and a cambric underlay. *White. Front Lengths:* 36 to 42 inches. For general wear this Petticoat is an ideal selection. **.55**

8A69—Handsome Petticoat of soft-finished Muslin. A deep flounce of embroidery in a rich openwork pattern trims this Petticoat. The upper part of the flounce is run with lustrous silk ribbon which ties in a pretty bow, as pictured. Draw-string in the waist-band. Muslin underlay. *White. Front Lengths:* 36 to 42 inches. This Petticoat will serve you on every occasion .. **$1.29**

8A67—Excellent quality White Longcloth Petticoat. A stylish double-ruffle flounce made of embroidery trims this attractive garment. A dainty ribbon-run beading heads the flounce, which has a serviceable underlay. Draw-string in the waist-band. *Front Lengths:* 36 to 42 inches. **$1.19**

8A96—The charming new *"Patricia"* Corset Cover of fine White Nainsook combined with Filet pattern lace and Val edging. Front and back alike. Elastic in the waist-band. *Sizes:* 32 to 46 bust.......... **.59**

8A71—Bands of exquisite lace and beautifully embroidered organdie form the deep flounce of this extra quality Muslin Petticoat. It is exceedingly dainty and rich-looking. A muslin underlay protects the flounce. Ribbon rosette. *White. Front Lengths:* 36 to 42 inches.... **$1.98**

Quality Petticoats For Women

8A72
79¢

8A103
$1.39
Camisole

8A76
$1.00

8A72—You will get good long service from this Petticoat. It is made of fine quality soft-finished Cambric with an embroidery flounce. A deep cambric underlay provides additional service. Wash silk ribbon is attractively drawn through the embroidery flounce and ties in a pretty bow, as pictured. Draw-string in the waist-band. *White. Front Lengths:* 36 to 42 inches. **.79**

8A76—A smooth-fitting, nicely made Petticoat of fine quality soft-finished Cambric. Flounce and ribbon-run heading of openwork embroidery in an exceptionally rich pattern. There is a draw-string in the waist-band. *White. Front Lengths:* 36 to 42 inches. You will get far more than $1.00's worth of satisfaction and service from this Petticoat...... **$1.00**

8A77
Set of Three
$1.49

8A73
89¢

8A74
$1.98

8A75
$1.39

8A103—Exquisite *"Grecian"* Camisole of lustrous Wash Satin and Filet pattern lace. Satin ribbon double shoulder straps. Elastic in the waist-band. *Colors:* flesh-pink or white. *Sizes:* 32 to 46 bust........ **$1.39**

8A74—This Petticoat is beautiful enough to wear with your finest costume. It is made of soft Muslin with a very deep flounce of handsome Imported Embroidery, headed with ribbon-run embroidery to match. Muslin underlay. Draw-string in the waist-band. *White. Front Lengths:* 36 to 42 inches. **$1.98**

Crinkled Crêpe Washes Snowy White and Requires No Ironing

8A73—Washable Crinkled Crêpe Petticoat. It is light in weight, smooth-fitting, cool, and altogether delightfully comfortable to wear during the Spring and Summer months. It is very easy to launder and does not have to be ironed. It is made with a deep flounce headed with ribbon-run lace beading and attractively finished with Irish crochet pattern lace. Draw-string in the waist-band. *White. Front Lengths:* 36 to 42 inches. **.89**

8A77—Order this three-piece Petticoat Set on our recommendation. Each Petticoat is neatly made of good quality Cambric with an attractive embroidery flounce with scalloped edge. Two of them are finished off with dainty ribbon rosettes, as pictured. Draw-strings in the waist-bands. *White. Front Lengths:* 36 to 42 inches. These Petticoats are worth 79 cents each. Sold only in Sets of 3 (one of each style) **$1.49**

8A75—A lovely Petticoat for dressy wear. The deep flounce made of Point de Paris lace and heavily embroidered organdie is very rich and effective. The upper part and the underlay are of soft white Muslin. Dainty ribbon rosette. *Front Lengths:* 36 to 42 inches..................... **$1.39**

OUR GUARANTEE IS ABSOLUTE—SATISFACTION ASSURED

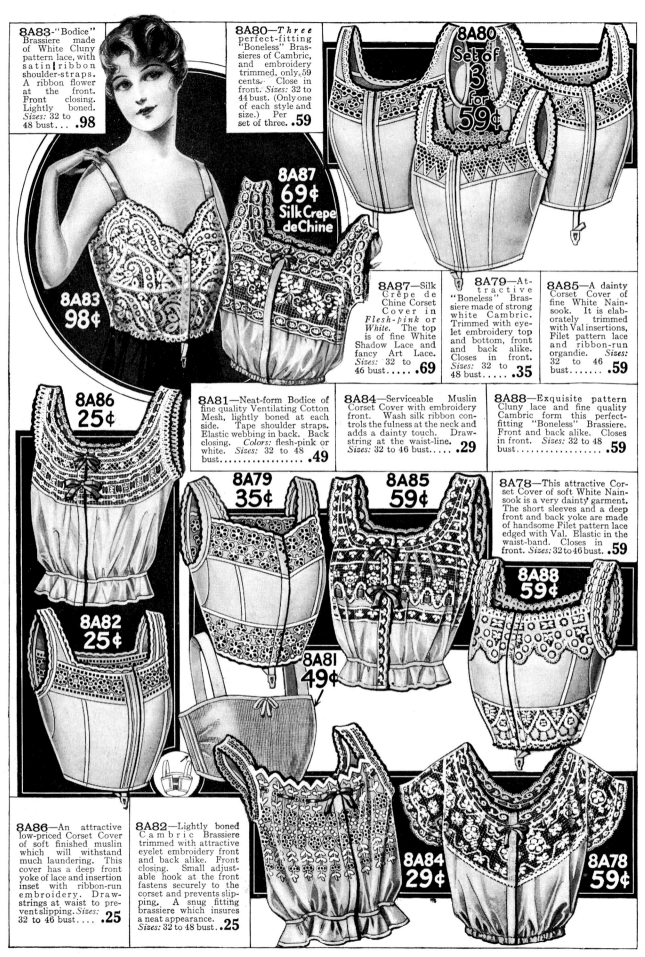

8A83—"Bodice" Brassiere made of White Cluny pattern lace, with satin ribbon shoulder-straps. A ribbon flower at the front. Front closing. Lightly boned. *Sizes:* 32 to 48 bust... **.98**

8A83
98¢

8A80—*Three* perfect-fitting "Boneless" Brassieres of Cambric, and embroidery trimmed, only, 59 cents. Close in front. *Sizes:* 32 to 44 bust. (Only one of each style and size.) Per set of three. **.59**

8A80 Set of 3 for 59¢

8A87 69¢ Silk Crepe de Chine

8A87—Silk Crêpe de Chine Corset Cover in *Flesh-pink* or *White.* The top is of fine White Shadow Lace and fancy Art Lace. *Sizes:* 32 to 46 bust..... **.69**

8A79—Attractive "Boneless" Brassiere made of strong white Cambric. Trimmed with eyelet embroidery top and bottom, front and back alike. Closes in front. *Sizes:* 32 to 48 bust.... **.35**

8A85—A dainty Corset Cover of fine White Nainsook. It is elaborately trimmed with Val insertions, Filet pattern lace and ribbon-run organdie. *Sizes:* 32 to 46 bust....... **.59**

8A86 25¢

8A81—Neat-form Bodice of fine quality Ventilating Cotton Mesh, lightly boned at each side. Tape shoulder straps. Elastic webbing in back. Back closing. *Colors:* flesh-pink or white. *Sizes:* 32 to 48 bust................. **.49**

8A84—Serviceable Muslin Corset Cover with embroidery front. Wash silk ribbon controls the fulness at the neck and adds a dainty touch. Drawstring at the waist-line. **.29**

8A88—Exquisite pattern Cluny lace and fine quality Cambric form this perfect-fitting "Boneless" Brassiere. Front and back alike. Closes in front. *Sizes:* 32 to 48 bust.................. **.59**

8A79 35¢

8A85 59¢

8A78—This attractive Corset Cover of soft White Nainsook is a very dainty garment. The short sleeves and a deep front and back yoke are made of handsome Filet pattern lace edged with Val. Elastic in the waist-band. Closes in front. *Sizes:* 32 to 46 bust. **.59**

8A82 25¢

8A88 59¢

8A81 49¢

8A86—An attractive low-priced Corset Cover of soft finished muslin which will withstand much laundering. This cover has a deep front yoke of lace and insertion inset with ribbon-run embroidery. Drawstrings at waist to prevent slipping. *Sizes:* 32 to 46 bust.... **.25**

8A82—Lightly boned Cambric Brassiere trimmed with attractive eyelet embroidery front and back alike. Front closing. Small adjustable hook at the front fastens securely to the corset and prevents slipping. A snug fitting brassiere which insures a neat appearance. *Sizes:* 32 to 48 bust. **.25**

8A84 29¢

8A78 59¢

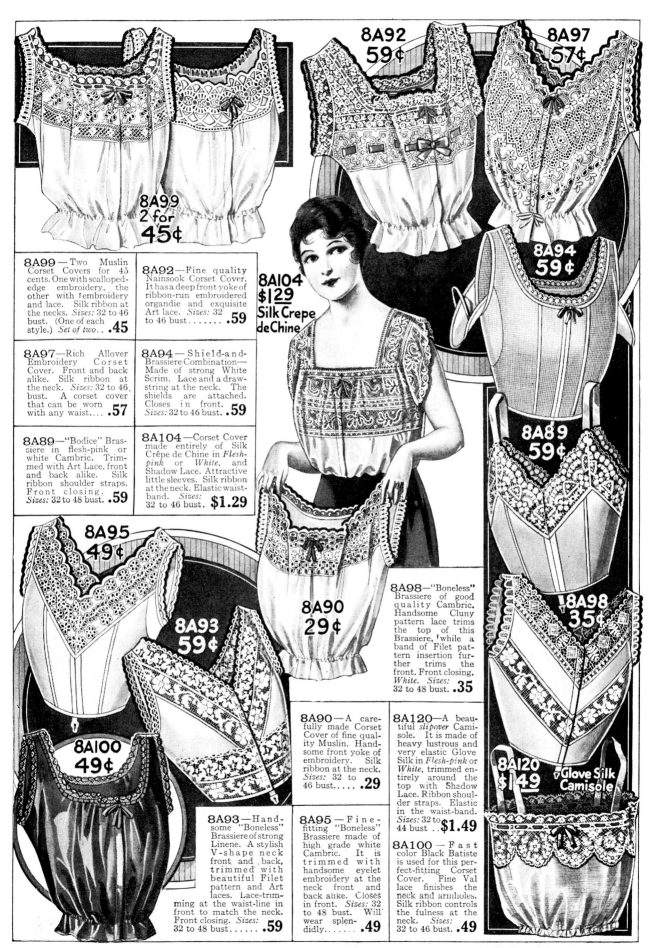

8A99 2 for 45¢

8A92 59¢

8A97 57¢

8A104 $1.29 Silk Crepe de Chine

8A94 59¢

8A89 59¢

8A95 49¢

8A93 59¢

8A100 49¢

8A90 29¢

8A98 35¢

8A120 $1.49 Glove Silk Camisole

8A99—Two Muslin Corset Covers for 45 cents. One with scalloped-edge embroidery, the other with ¡embroidery and lace. Silk ribbon at the necks. Sizes: 32 to 46 bust. (One of each style.) *Set of two*.. **.45**

8A92—Fine quality Nainsook Corset Cover. It has a deep front yoke of ribbon-run embroidered organdie and exquisite Art lace. *Sizes: 32 to 46 bust*....... **.59**

8A97—Rich Allover Embroidery Corset Cover. Front and back alike. Silk ribbon at the necks. *Sizes: 32 to 46. bust*. A corset cover that can be worn with any waist.... **.57**

8A94—Shield-and-Brassiere Combination—Made of strong White Scrim. Lace and a drawstring at the neck. The shields are attached. Closes in front. *Sizes: 32 to 46 bust*. **.59**

8A89—"Bodice" Brassiere in flesh-pink or white Cambric. Trimmed with Art Lace, front and back alike. Silk ribbon shoulder straps. Front closing. *Sizes: 32 to 48 bust*. **.59**

8A104—Corset Cover made entirely of Silk Crêpe de Chine in *Flesh-pink* or *White*, and Shadow Lace. Attractive little sleeves. Silk ribbon at the neck. Elastic waistband. *Sizes: 32 to 46 bust*. **$1.29**

8A98—"Boneless" Brassiere of good quality Cambric. Handsome Cluny pattern lace trims the top of this Brassiere, while a band of Filet pattern insertion further trims the front. Front closing. White. Sizes: 32 to 48 bust. **.35**

8A90—A carefully made Corset Cover of fine quality Muslin. Handsome front yoke of embroidery. Silk ribbon at the neck. *Sizes: 32 to 46 bust*..... **.29**

8A120—A beautiful *slipover* Camisole. It is made of heavy lustrous and very elastic Glove Silk in *Flesh-pink* or *White*, trimmed entirely around the top with Shadow Lace. Ribbon shoulder straps. Elastic in the waist-band. *Sizes: 32 to 44 bust* ..**$1.49**

8A93—Handsome "Boneless" Brassiere of strong Linene. A stylish V-shape neck front and back, trimmed with beautiful Filet pattern and Art laces. Lace-trimming at the waist-line in front to match the neck. Front closing. *Sizes: 32 to 48 bust*...... **.59**

8A95—Fine-fitting "Boneless" Brassiere made of high grade white Cambric. It is trimmed with handsome eyelet embroidery at the neck front and back alike. Closes in front. *Sizes: 32 to 48 bust*. Will wear splendidly....... **.49**

8A100—Fast color Black Batiste is used for this perfect-fitting Corset Cover. Fine Val lace finishes the neck and armholes. Silk ribbon controls the fulness at the neck. *Sizes: 32 to 46 bust*. **.49**

8A106—Girls' Princess Slip made of soft White Nainsook. Embroidery and silk baby ribbon trim this petticoat. Lace-trimmed armholes. Buttons in back. *Sizes:* 6 to 14 years.................**.57**

8A119 45¢

8A113 29¢

8A112 15¢

8A111 25¢ up

8A107 29¢

8A119—Misses' and Girls' Bloomer-Drawers of soft White Crinkled Crêpe. Elastic at the waist-band and knees. Closed. *Sizes:* 14 to 18 years.......**.45**

8A113—Misses' and Girls' Drawers of fine White Muslin trimmed with pin-tucks and handsome embroidery ruffles. Buttonholed waist-band. Closed. *Sizes:* 14 to 18 years.......**.29**

8A112—Muslin Drawers with pin-tucks. *Sizes:* 2 to 12 years. Buttonholed waist-band. Closed...**.15**

8A111—Cambric knickers, embroidery trimmed. Buttonholed waist-band. Closed. *Sizes:* 2 to 6 years.**.25** 8 to 12 years.**.29**

8A117 29¢

8A118 30¢ up

8A116 2 for 29¢

8A106 57¢

8A107—Little Girls' Petticoat of soft White Cambric, trimmed with dainty embroidery ruffle. Closes in back. *Sizes:* 2 to 6 years **.29**

8A117—Drawers-waist of White Cambric trimmed with lace at the neck and armholes. Back closing. *Sizes:* 2 to 12. Each.............**.29**

8A118—Crêpe bloomer-drawers. Elastic at the knees. Buttonholed waist-band. Closed. *Sizes:* 2 to 6 years..**.30** *Sizes:* 8 to 12.............**.35**

8A116—Cambric Drawers-waist. Back closing. *Sizes:* 2 to 12. Two for.**.29**

8A115—Girls' dressy Petticoat of fine quality Muslin. It is trimmed with pin-tucks and handsome ribbon-run embroidery, as pictured. *Sizes:* 4 to 14 years. Will wear splendidly.....**.45**

8A109 59¢

8A105—Serviceable Muslin Nightgown. It is prettily trimmed with embroidery, lace and ribbon. The short sleeves and low neck make it delightfully cool. Cut full and roomy.
Sizes: 2 to 6 years.................**.59**
Sizes: 8 to 14 years...............**.65**

8A105 59¢ up

8A115 45¢

8A110 19¢

8A114 29¢

8A108 39¢

8A110—Infant's Diaper Drawers of strong White Muslin with an embroidery edging. Buttonholed waist-band. A practical and comfortable garment for every little child. **.19**

8A114—Attractive Petticoat of soft-finished Cambric, with flounce of embroidery and pin-tucks. *Sizes:* 2 to 12 years. A splendid garment for service..........**.29**

8A108—Child's Sleeping Garment made of serviceable White Cambric. Drop seat. Closes in back. *Sizes:* 2 to 6 years. A comfortable Sleeping Garment. It is perfectly cut and proportioned..................**.39**

8A109—Child's Combination—Waist and Knickerbocker Drawers. It is made of soft White Muslin, prettily trimmed with ribbon-run embroidery, as pictured. Drop seat. Closes in back. *Sizes:* 2 to 6 years.....**.59**

PERRY, DAME & CO.

142 to 154 East 32nd Street, New York City

Please send the following goods for which I enclose $.......

(Be sure to register your letter if it contains cash or stamps)

The Perry-Dame Guarantee

It is agreed by Perry, Dame & Co. that they will pay all delivery charges, and if, for any reason whatever, I am not entirely pleased with these goods, I may return them either to be exchanged for other goods, or I may have my money refunded, without one cent of expense to me.

(Read GUARANTEE on inside front cover, page 2)

PLEASE DO NOT WRITE IN THIS SPACE
M. O.   C
Ch.   St.

Mrs.
or Miss..............................

Street, R. F. D.
or Box Number..........................

Post Office...........................

State...............................

Style No.	How Many	Color	Bust, or Size	Waist	Length	ARTICLE	PRICE $	Cts.
Style No.	How many	Color	Bust, or Size	Waist	Length	Article		
Style No.	How many	Color	Bust, or Size	Waist	Length	Article		
Style No.	How many	Color	Bust, or Size	Waist	Length	Article		
Style No.	How many	Color	Bust, or Size	Waist	Length	Article		
Style No.	How many	Color	Bust, or Size	Waist	Length	Article		
Style No.	How many	Color	Bust, or Size	Waist	Length	Article		
Style No.	How many	Color	Bust, or Size	Waist	Length	Article		
Style No.	How many	Color	Bust, or Size	Waist	Length	Article		
Style No.	How many	Color	Bust, or Size	Waist	Length	Article		
Style No.	How many	Color	Bust, or Size	Waist	Length	Article		
Style No.	How many	Color	Bust, or Size	Waist	Length	Article		
Style No.	How many	Color	Bust, or Size	Waist	Length	Article		
Style No.	How many	Color	Bust, or Size	Waist	Length	Article		
Style No.	How many	Color	Bust, or Size	Waist	Length	Article		
						TOTAL		

Will you read this order over again? Be sure you have given correct style number, correct color, and all necessary measurements.

WE WANT TO FILL YOUR ORDER EXACTLY RIGHT

(OVER)

A Few Simple Directions for Ordering

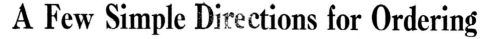

We want to fill your order exactly right, so we ask you to please read this page carefully.

Perry-Dame Clothes always fit you perfectly if you order the right size garment. And it is a very easy matter for you to find out just what size garment you should wear—that is, by actually taking your measurement with an accurate tape measure.

To find your correct BUST MEASURE, take an accurate tape measure and your size will be the number of inches over the largest part of bust, taken over your shirtwaist. (See illustration.) Be sure that the tape measure does not slip up or down in the back and do not take this measurement too tight. Make no allowances whatever.

To find your correct WAIST MEASURE, take this measurement all around your waist, making no allowances.

To find your correct HIP MEASURE, take this measurement all around your hips about six inches below your waist-line, making no allowances.

When ordering SKIRTS, either with a regulation waist-band or girdle top, give your waist measure taken around your waist, making no allowances; and also give front length, taken from waist-line to desired length as shown in the picture between points "A" and "B."

How to Order Your Right Sizes

WOMEN'S DRESSES

Women's Dresses come in sizes 32 to 46 bust, with the skirt 40 inches in length, made with a deep basted hem, so they can be easily shortened or lengthened by the customer if desired.

Send us your actual bust and waist measures and we will send you the right size. If you wish you may also send us your hip measure as an additional guide.

WOMEN'S COATS

Take your Bust Measure over your shirtwaist with an accurate tape measure, making no allowance and we will send you your right size. The length of each coat is stated in each description.

WOMEN'S SUITS

Women's Suits come from 32 to 46 inches bust, and the skirt length is 40 inches with a deep basted hem for easy adjustment.

Send us your bust measure and your waist measure and we will send you your right size. You may, if you like, also send us your hip measure as an additional guide.

CORSETS

It is an easy matter for you to get a perfect-fitting Corset at Perry, Dame & Co.'s. Order by Size, not by waist measure. The correct size of a regular Corset (also Reducing and Maternity models) is three inches less than your waist measure taken over your dress. Topless Corsets and Misses' Corset Waists should be ordered TWO INCHES smaller than your waist measure taken over your dress. Front-lacing Corsets should be ordered ONE INCH smaller than your waist measure taken over your dress.

SHOES

Read how to order your right size shoes on page 91.

MISSES' DRESSES

Misses' Dresses come in sizes 14 to 20 years, in accordance with the following schedule:

14 years, bust 32 inches; skirt length 31 inches.
16 years, bust 34 inches; skirt length 33 inches.
18 years, bust 36 inches; skirt length 35 inches.
20 years, bust 38 inches; skirt length 37 inches.

All skirts made with deep basted hem for easy adjustment. Order the Size that comes nearest to your measurements, or give us your exact bust measure and we will send you your right size.

MISSES' COATS

Misses' Coats come in sizes 14 to 20 years, in accordance with the following schedule:

14 years, 32 bust.
16 years, 34 bust.
18 years, 36 bust.
20 years, 38 bust.

The length of each coat is stated in the description.

Take your bust measurement over your shirtwaist, and then order the size that comes nearest to that measurement.

MISSES' SUITS

Misses' Suits come in sizes 14 to 20 years, in accordance with the following schedule:

14 years, bust 32 inches; skirt length 31 inches.
16 years, bust 34 inches; skirt length 33 inches.
18 years, bust 36 inches; skirt length 35 inches.
20 years, bust 38 inches; skirt length 37 inches

Deep basted hem for easy adjustment.

PETTICOATS

Be sure to order petticoats two inches shorter than the front length of your skirt, as this is the right length in order to get the best effect and the greatest amount of service.

SIZE SCALES FOR JUNIORS
13, 15 and 17 Years
SUITS AND DRESSES

13 years, bust 33 inches; skirt length 31 inches.
15 years, bust 35 inches; skirt length 32 inches.
17 years, bust 37 inches; skirt length 34 inches.

COATS

13 years, 33 bust.
15 years, 35 bust.
17 years, 37 bust.

Lengths correctly proportioned to correspond. Order by the age that is nearest to the young misses' bust measure.

SIZE SCALES FOR GIRLS' DRESSES
6 to 14 Years

Size	Chest	Length
6 years	26 inches	26 inches
8 years	28 inches	30 inches
10 years	30 inches	34 inches
12 years	32 inches	38 inches
14 years	34 inches	42 inches

GLOVES

If you know what size glove you wear, and it is the right size for you, order your new gloves by that size. If you are not sure of your size, take a tape measure and measure around the knuckles as shown in this picture. Draw the tape close, but not too tight. The number of inches is the size of the gloves. Do not order gloves too tight. If your hand measures 6⅜ inches, order size 6½, and so on.

PERRY, DAME & CO.

142 to 154 East 32nd Street, New York City

Please send the following goods for which I enclose $. . . . . . .

(Be sure to register your letter if it contains cash or stamps)

The Perry-Dame Guarantee

It is agreed by Perry, Dame & Co. that they will pay all delivery charges, and if, for any reason whatever, I am not entirely pleased with these goods, I may return them either to be exchanged for other goods, or I may have my money refunded, without one cent of expense to me.

(Read GUARANTEE on inside front cover, page 2)

PLEASE DO NOT WRITE IN THIS SPACE
M. O.   C
Ch.   St.

Mrs.
or Miss. . . . .

Street, R. F. D.
or Box Number. . . . .

Post Office. . . . .

State. . . . .

Style No.	How Many	Color	Bust, or Size	Waist	Length	ARTICLE	PRICE $	Cts.
Style No.	How many	Color	Bust, or Size	Waist	Length	Article		
Style No.	How many	Color	Bust, or Size	Waist	Length	Article		
Style No.	How many	Color	Bust, or Size	Waist	Length	Article		
Style No.	How many	Color	Bust, or Size	Waist	Length	Article		
Style No.	How many	Color	Bust, or Size	Waist	Length	Article		
Style No.	How many	Color	Bust, or Size	Waist	Length	Article		
Style No.	How many	Color	Bust, or Size	Waist	Length	Article		
Style No.	How many	Color	Bust, or Size	Waist	Length	Article		
Style No.	How many	Color	Bust, or Size	Waist	Length	Article		
Style No.	How many	Color	Bust, or Size	Waist	Length	Article		
Style No.	How many	Color	Bust, or Size	Waist	Length	Article		
Style No.	How many	Color	Bust, or Size	Waist	Length	Article		
Style No.	How many	Color	Bust, or Size	Waist	Length	Article		
Style No.	How many	Color	Bust, or Size	Waist	Length	Article		
						TOTAL		

Will you read this order over again? Be sure you have given correct style number, correct color, and all necessary measurements.

WE WANT TO FILL YOUR ORDER EXACTLY RIGHT

(OVER)

Quality Always Counts

We believe that and because we believe it and know it to be true, we have kept that thought foremost in our minds in the making of this catalog.

The illustrations in this book do not do full justice to the merchandise we have selected and have on our shelves.

The illustrations can only show you the attractiveness of the style and the beauty of design and pattern. The pictures cannot show you the careful workmanship and the quality of the material which enters into the garments we now have to fill your orders.

For the reason that we cannot snow this quality and workmanship in the pictures, we want to say to you now as forcibly as we can that in all our selecting and buying, Quality and Value has been the first consideration.

We might have selected cheaper merchandise which might look as good in a picture. We have not done that. We have selected the *best* merchandise—merchandise that will satisfy you so well that you will order all your wearing apparel from the firm of Perry, Dame & Co. We want your confidence, your respect and your patronage.

Undoubtedly there is something in these pages that you need *now*. Use the convenient order blanks in this book; send us your order for what you need. You will not only be satisfied, but you will be glad you made the purchase.

Perry Dame & Co.

Two Striking Costumes

for OUT-OF-DOOR WEAR

9A53
$1⁷⁹

HAT 7A53
$1⁶⁹

5A1
$5⁹⁸

1A601
$7⁹⁸

9A53—Smart Appearing, Waist. Slight gathers on tendency to severity. Sleeves show pointed turned-back cuffs of the material. *Colors:* Tan, rose or white. well tailored Tussah Silk the shoulder seams offset, any Patch pockets at either side. *Sizes:* 32 to 46 bust measure.............................. **$1.79**

5A1—Extremely Well Made Skirt of All Wool Novelty Serge. It embodies all the latest style features. Note the smooth-fitting belt cut in pointed yoke effect, trimmed with smoked pearl buttons. The patch pockets have two deep points and gathers accomplished by means of buttons. Front closing with large pearl buttons. *Colors:* Black or blue stripes on white ground. *Sizes:* Waist measures 22 to 30 inches; front lengths, 36 to 43 inches. **$5.98**

7A53—Sport Hat of Fine Quality Panama, with up-turned brim at one side and round crown. Trimmed with black velvet band, caught with black button...... **$1.69**

1A601—Misses' Striking Costume of Superior Quality Sport Crêpe. Suitable for afternoon wear at beach or mountain resorts. The yoke forms deep points at either side of the simulated double front closing. Below the yoke, the plaits are adjusted by the new "throw-tie" belt, with tasseled ends. The skirt is of Awning Striped Sport Crêpe and falls in graceful box plaits to the hem. The Middy is plain white Sport Crêpe, with collar, cuffs and belt of the Awning Striped material in navy and gold or Copenhagen and red to match the skirt. Silk tie at neck. *Sizes:* 14, 16, 18 and 20 years.... **$7.98**

STUNNING SWEATERS FOR SUMMER WEAR

16A2 $5.00

16A3 $5.69

16A1 $10.98

16A1—Remarkably Beautiful Dress Sweater of Pure Fibre Silk. Fibre Silk is famous for its rich appearance and excellent wearing qualities. The back is gracefully shirred on elastic bands, as shown in the small back view. The deep, square-back collar is a pleasing feature of this sweater. The gathered pockets are roomy and unusual. Novel sash belt. The closing is effected with ivory-rimmed buttons and silk cord loops. *Colors:* Copenhagen blue, rose or gold. *Sizes:* 32 to 44 bust measure. The lustrous material and smartness of the design make this garment unusually desirable.. **$10.98**

16A2—Extremely Fashionable New Model Sweater of All Worsted in Shetland Stitch. This sweater is delightfully soft and elastic. It is light in weight, yet warm. The deep collar and belt are of White Angora Wool. The pockets are also trimmed with Angora. Self covered buttons and loops form the closing. *Colors:* Copenhagen blue, rose or gold, each with white trimming. *Sizes:* 32 to 44 bust measure................................... **$5.00**

16A3—Handsome All Wool Jersey Cloth Sport Coat. The wide attractive belt encircling the back is finished in front with sash ends. These may be detached when desired simply by unbuttoning them at the side. The deep collar with its notched revers and the cuffs are of White All Wool Jersey. The pockets are finished with the White Jersey trimming. *Colors:* Copenhagen blue or rose. *Sizes:* 32 to 44 bust measure............................ **$5.69**

PERRY, DAME & CO., 142 to 154 EAST 32nd ST., NEW YORK CITY

[original back cover]